MW01193189

A DoD CCRP/NDU Collaboration

This collaborative effort is a continuation of the series of publications produced by the Center for Advanced Concepts and Technology (ACT), which was created as a "skunk works" with funding provided by the Assistant Secretary of Defense (C3I). The early success of ACT led to the creation of ACTIS when the president of the National Defense University (NDU) merged the experimental School of Information Warfare and Strategy with ACT and ASD (C3I) made the Director of ACTIS the executive agent for the DoD Command and Control Research Program (CCRP). ACTIS has demonstrated the importance of having a research program focused on the national security implications of the Information Age and in providing the theoretical foundations for providing DoD with information superiority, as well as the importance of an educational program designed to acquaint senior military personnel and civilians with these emerging issues. As a result, ACTIS's educational programs are being merged with the Colleges of NDU and ACTIS's research programs are being transitioned to OSD under the direction of ASD (C3I).

DoD Command and Control Research Program

Assistant Secretary of Defense (C3I)
    Mr. Anthony Valletta (Acting)
Deputy Assistant Secretary of Defense (C3I) Acquisition
    Dr. Margaret Myers (Acting)
Executive Agent for CCRP
    Dr. David S. Alberts
    Mr. Larry Wentz* (Acting)

Library of Congress Cataloging-in-Publication Data

Combelles-Siegel, Pascale.
    Target Bosnia : integrating information activities in peace operations :
NATO-led operations in Bosnia-Herzegovina, December 1995-1997 / Pascale
Combelles Siegel.
        p. cm.
    Includes bibliographical references.
    ISBN 1-57906-008-0
    1. Yugoslav War, 1991- --Press coverage. 2. Yugoslav War, 1991- --Mass
media and the war. 3. Yugoslav War, 1991- --Propaganda. 4. Yugoslav War,
1991- --Bosnia and Hercegovina. 5. North Atlantic Treaty Organization.   I.
Title.
DR1313.7.P73C66 1998   98-13326
949.703--dc21   CIP

*as of January 1998

The National Defense University

The Institute for National Strategic Studies (INSS) is a major component of the National Defense University (NDU) that operates under the supervision of the President of NDU. It conducts strategic studies for the Secretary of Defense, Chairman of the Joint Chiefs of Staff, and unified commanders in chief; supports national strategic components of NDU academic programs; and provides outreach to other governmental agencies and the broader national security community.

The Publication Directorate of INSS publishes books, monographs, reports, and occasional papers on national security strategy, defense policy, and national military strategy through NDU Press that reflect the output of NDU research and academic programs. In addition, it produces the INSS Strategic Assessment and other work approved by the President of NDU as well as *Joint Force Quarterly*, a professional military journal published for the Chairman, Joint Chiefs of Staff.

Target Bosnia: Integrating Information Activities in Peace Operations

NATO-Led Operations In Bosnia-Herzegovina
December 1995-1997

Pascale Combelles Siegel

Acknowledgments

This project was made possible through a grant from NATO Individual Research Fellowship and the sponsorship of Evidence Based Research, Inc. (EBR) and the National Defense University (NDU). The French Service d'Information et de Relations Publiques des Armées (SIRPA) facilitated a three-week observation trip to Bosnia-Herzegovina in October 1996. The author returned to Bosnia-Herzegovina under NATO auspices in March-April 1997.

Many people assisted in this study, agreeing to interviews, providing documents, and reviewing portions of this monograph. The author greatly appreciates this support, without which the study would have been impossible. In particular, I want to thank my husband, Adam B. Siegel, for his assistance and advice. In the end, the author bears full responsibility for any faults that remain. The views expressed within are the author's and do not necessarily represent official views of NDU (U.S. Government), SIRPA (French government), or NATO.

Table of Contents

Introduction

"No matter how brilliantly you fight, what matters
is the actual packaging."[1]

With each day that passes drawing us further down the path from the Industrial to the Information Age, many officers are convinced that victory is no longer determined on the ground, but in media reporting. This is even more true in peace support operations (PSO) where the goal is not to conquer territory or defeat an enemy but to persuade parties in conflict (as well as the local populations) into a favored course of action. This monograph examines the role of information in PSO and its impact on command and control through the prism of NATO-led operations in Bosnia-Herzegovina from December 1995 into 1997.

Following the signing on 14 December 1995 of the Dayton Peace Agreement, which put an end to a four-year war in Bosnia-Herzegovina, the UN mandated NATO to oversee and enforce a durable cease-fire between

---

[1] Lawry Philips, chief media operations at the Permanent Joint Headquarters (PJHQ). Interview with the author, PJHQ, Northwood, UK, 12 August 1997. The PJHQ is (approximately) the UK equivalent of the U.S. Joint Chiefs of Staff.

the former belligerents.² On 20 December 1995, a NATO-led multinational force called the Implementation Force (IFOR) started *Operation Joint Endeavour*. On 20 December 1996, a smaller NATO coalition called the Stabilization Force (SFOR) replaced IFOR. In *Operation Joint Guard*, SFOR received an 18-month mandate to oversee and enforce the cease-fire.

In Bosnia, IFOR and then SFOR ran an information campaign designed to "seize and maintain the initiative by imparting timely and effective information within the commander's intent."³ The term "information campaign" refers to the coordinated and synchronized use of different information activities within the command. The campaign had three components.

- A public information (PI) campaign designed to establish NATO's credibility with the international media to gain support from the contributing nations for the mission. Public Information Officers executed this mission.

---

² This came after over three years of NATO operations related to the war in Bosnia. Since July 92, NATO naval forces had monitored (and then enforced starting in November) the UN arms embargo (Operation SHARP GUARD). Since October 92, NATO forces had monitored (and then enforced starting in April 1993) the UN-imposed no-fly zone over Bosnia (Operation DENY FLIGHT). In June 1993, NATO offered close air support to the United Nations Protection Force (UNPROFOR). Problems in the command and control arrangements for this close air support heavily influenced the structure for the international implementation of the DPA starting in December 1995. Starting 30 August 1995, NATO executed operation DELIBERATE FORCE, a series of air strikes against Bosnian Serb military targets. For a discussion of NATO and the UN operations in the Former Republics of Yugoslavia, see: Dick A. Leudijk, "Before and After Dayton: The UN and NATO in the former Yugoslavia," *Third World Quarterly*, vol. 18, no 3, 1997, pp. 457-470; Gregory L. Schulte, "Former Yugoslavia and New NATO," *Survival*, vol. 39, no 1, Spring 1997, pp. 19-42.

³ Col. Tim Wilton, UKA, ARRC Chief Information Officer (CIO), Sarajevo, 12 October 1996. Although this definition applied principally to IFOR operations, it also seemed to accurately reflect what SFOR did.

- A psychological operations (PSYOP) campaign designed to influence the local population and its leaders in favor of IFOR troops and operations. PSYOP units (mainly American) undertook this aspect of the campaign.
- A Civil-Military Cooperation (CIMIC) information campaign designed to inform audiences about civil-military cooperation and to release information to aid the local populations. CIMIC elements (mainly U.S. Army) undertook this mission.

In this monograph, information activities refers to the different components of the campaign, and information campaign refers to the coordination of the various elements. This terminology was adopted in part to avoid confusion with a new fashionable term: information operations. According to the U.S. Army's Field Manual, FM 100-6, information operations refers to operations linking together public affairs, civil affairs, psychological operations, command and control warfare, and electronic warfare. Such all-encompassing information operations did not take place during NATO-led operations in Bosnia.[4]

During the planning of *Operation Joint Endeavour*, NATO commanders and political leadership thought that information activities would make a critical contribution to mission accomplishment. In particular, they expected a successful public information campaign to contribute to building and preserving public support for the mili-

---

[4] Department of the Army, *Field Manual: FM 100-6: Information Operations*, Washington, D.C.

tary operation. Indeed, media reporting affects how the world and the local communities assess the events of peace operations, as it provides the basis for the world's—including many in the political elite—judgment as to the success or failure of a peace operation. As the main interface between the command and journalists, the public information officers' role was deemed crucial.

Information activities were also expected to help commanders communicate to the parties their intentions and might and to lead the local population to act friendly. During both the United Nations Protection Force (UNPROFOR) and NATO operations in Bosnia, major military operations were rare.[5] On the other hand, IFOR (and later SFOR) often used information activities to deter the Bosnian factions from violating the military annex of the Dayton agreement and from attacking NATO troops. IFOR/SFOR also used information activities to convince the local population that a brighter future would await them if the Dayton agreement was fully complied with.

Before the NATO deployment began in December 1995, the stakes were particularly high for a successful information campaign. After the doomed UNPROFOR mission (widely perceived, especially in the United States,

---

[5] During UN and NATO missions through mid-1997, major military operations were rare. One of them took place in March 1996, when IFOR seized arms and ammunitions from the Bosniac government. IFOR also seized many documents linking the Bosniac government to Iran. Another major operation occurred when SFOR troops redeployed in Republika Srpska to back the elected President Biljana Plavsic in her power struggle against the Bosnian-Serb military leader Radovan Karadzic (summer 1997). Karadzic, an indicted war criminal, gave up all official positions in 1996 under pressure from the international community. However, although unofficially, he retained substantial influence on the Bosnian Serb republic politics and economics.

as a dramatic failure), a success or failure of the NATO mission was of utmost importance for the future of peacekeeping operations and for the credibility of collective security. As the first NATO ground military operation and largest UN operation ever, the success or failure of NATO operations in Bosnia-Herzegovina may determine the fate of UN and NATO peace operations for years to come. In consequence, it was of utmost importance that the mission be well explained to and well understood by the public at large and elite around the world. As the main interface between the public and the commanders, public information played a decisive role in this process. If the public information campaign contributed to the success of NATO's operations in Bosnia-Herzegovina, it might mean significant developments in attitudes toward and possibilities for pursuit of peace operations. On the other hand, a failure of the operation, and of its public information effort, might provide one more reason not to engage in such operations in the future.

Political tensions in the United States also complicated the situation, with Congress reluctant to send U.S. ground forces to what many perceived as a quagmire in the making and the U.S. public always ambivalent about long-term commitments. Throughout the Dayton negotiation, partisans and opponents hotly debated whether U.S. ground troops should go to Bosnia as guarantor of the process. When the Clinton Administration decided in Fall 1995 that time was finally ripe for decisive political action in the region, it was well aware of the inherent dangers of its interventionist policy. To succeed, the policy had to be seen as successful and its merits needed to be well explained to the governing elite (especially in Congress) and the U.S. public.

Successful information activities were all the more important since propaganda had played a leading role in forging the war and justifying atrocities and crimes throughout the four-year conflict. "From the war's outbreak, the media in former Yugoslavia mostly published and broadcast nationalist discourses, attacks and other general insults directed against other ethnic groups. It is not surprising that this led directly to horrible atrocities on battlefields and throughout the territory."[6] Across Bosnia, the media became the loyal instruments of the factions' policies of war, ethnic purification, and atrocities. The people's horizons shrank as the media portrayed reality in simplistic, black and white terms; demonized other ethnic groups (by inventing or exaggerating crimes or responsibilities); and offered simplistic explanations for a complex and ambivalent reality. No alternate viewpoint to the official party line was allowed. With few exceptions, the people of Bosnia were not provided with an honest picture of the unfolding events. Although the war stopped, the umbilical cord between the media and the dominating political parties was not

---

[6] Tadeusz Mazowiecki, "Depuis le début des conflits, les informations diffusées par les médias de l'ex-Yougoslavie ont consisté pour l'essentiel en discours nationalistes et en attaques et insultes généralisées dirigées contre les autres peuples. Il n'est pas surprenant que ce phénomène ait conduit directement à la perpétration d'horribles atrocités sur les champs de bataille et dans l'ensemble du territoire," in *Rapport spécial sur les médias*, Rapporteur spécial désigné par la résolution 1994/72 de la Commission des Droits de l'Homme des Nations Unies, E/CN 4/1995/54, 13 décembre 1994, p. 35.

severed. There may have been some changes in the prevalent news discourse, but these only reflected changing official tactics, and as such were very limited.[7]

With this complex background in mind, this monograph examines the place of PI and PSYOP in peace operations through the prism of NATO operations in Bosnia-Herzegovina. The monograph first presents a background on NATO-led operations in Bosnia, then analyzes the three pillars of the campaign: public information, psychological operations, and civil-military co-operation information. It then examines how these different tasks were coordinated throughout the command and with international organizations. The final section provides an assessment of the effectiveness of NATO information activities in support of mission accomplishment and offers some thoughts for future operations.

---

[7] Renaud de la Brosse, "Les voix de la guerre," in Général Jean Cot (ed.), *Dernière Guerre Balkanique ? Ex-Yougoslavie : Témoignages, analyses, perspectives*, Paris, Fondations pour les Etudes de Défense, l'Harmattan, 1996, pp. 165-181.

Chapter 1:
Background on
Operations in Bosnia

Operation *Joint Endeavour* began on 20 December 1995 after the Bosniac, Serb, and Croat factions (also called the Former Warring Factions, or FWF) agreed to a peace agreement that would end the four-year-long war and ethnic cleansing. Representatives from the Republic of Bosnia-Herzegovina (represented by Alia Izetbegovic), the Bosno-Croat Federation, and Republika Srpska (Bosno-Serbs), along with the Presidents of Croatia (Fanjo Tudjman) and the Federal Republic of Yugoslavia (Slobodan Milosevic)— referred to as the parties in the accord—negotiated the General Framework Agreement For Peace (GFAP) in Dayton, Ohio, and formally signed it in Paris on 14 December 1995.[8] The accord is commonly referred to as the Dayton Peace Agreement (DPA). It provided the structure and mandates for an international mission

---

[8] Milosevic signed the agreement on behalf of the Bosnian Serb leaders who had consistently refused the agreement. Milosevic had enough leverage on the situation to obtain their compliance.

9

designed to end the fighting and help the FWF achieve reconciliation under a unified, democratic, and multi-ethnic Bosnia.[9]

Summary of Main Responsibilities

The DPA lays down the responsibilities of the parties and the international community. The Bosniacs, Bosnian Croats, and Bosnian Serbs are mostly responsible for implementing the agreement. International organizations, with the notable exception of NATO, only have a facilitating role as supervisors and coordinators. According to the DPA, only NATO has the power to enforce the provisions of the agreement in case of non-compliance.

Ending the fighting was the fundamental prerequisite for a true reconciliation process to take place. Accordingly, annex 1A of the agreement tasked NATO with ensuring a "durable cessation of hostilities," monitoring and enforcing the separation of FWF's forces and the cantonment of their heavy weapons. The parties also agreed to release their prisoners of war under International Committee of the Red Cross (ICRC) supervision. To consolidate regional peace, the parties agreed to an arms reduction program designed to achieve a stable military balance in the region. Annex 1B of the agree-

---

[9] Observers criticized the agreement as soon as it was signed. See for example, Général Jean Cot, interview with LCI (French 24 hours news TV channel), 9 January 1996, transcript held at the SIRPA Documentation Center, Paris. The implementation process did not silence the critics. See Général Jean Cot, "Dayton: une paix bâclée," *Défense Nationale*, July 1997; and Dusko Doder, "Bosnia's False Peace: Psychologically and practically, all sides are preparing for war," *The Washington Post*, 16 March 1997, p. C7.

ment tasked the Organization for Security and Cooperation in Europe (OSCE) with assisting the parties to downsize their military forces (to the lowest level consistent with their respective security) and achieve regional stability. [10]

A key element in the international community's peace plan was the resurrection of Bosnia-Herzegovina as a unified country. At Dayton, the parties agreed to a single, democratic, and multi-ethnic Bosnia-Herzegovina (within the borders recognized by the international community in 1992). The new B-H is a federation made up of two entities: the (Bosno-Croat) Federation and the Republic of the Bosnian-Serbs (Republika Srpska). [11] In annex 3 of the DPA, the parties invited the OSCE to organize and supervise free and fair democratic elections within the first nine months after force entry (on 20 December 1995). The parties also agreed to a new constitutional framework establishing a federal regime based on two-to-one representation between the two entities—the Bosno-Croat Federation (2) and the Republika Srpska (1)—(annex 4). To foster democratic principles in B-H, the international community sponsored several programs. As part of this endeavor, the parties invited a UN-led International Police Task Force (IPTF) to monitor local police's activities and develop training programs in consultation with local authorities (annex 11). In the course of the operations, the IPTF received

---

[10] Appendix 1 presents a table summarizing the international organizations and the parties' responsibilities in implementing the DPA.

[11] See map of Bosnia-Herzegovina, as agreed upon in Dayton, in Appendix 2.

additional missions. At the London Peace Implementation Conference (December 1996), the international community tasked the IPTF with monitoring and investigating local police abuses.[12] In February 1997, the arbitration agreement on Brcko called for the IPTF to monitor, restructure, and retrain the local police to an extent far beyond that in any other parts of the country. In an effort to promote further democratization, several organizations, such as the OHR and the OSCE (as well as numerous non-governmental and governmental agencies), pursued media democratization.

Resolution of the lingering crisis in Bosnia-Herzegovina also required that people who fled during the war (refugees across Europe and displaced persons within Bosnia-Herzegovina) could return safely. At Dayton, the parties agreed that all Displaced Persons and Refugees (DPREs) were entitled to return wherever they chose (including their pre-war settlement), and recover their property as of 1991. In annex 7, the parties called for the United Nations High Commissioner for Refugees (UNHCR) to develop, in close consultation with the parties and the asylum countries, a repatriation plan for "early, orderly and peaceful return of refugees and displaced persons."

---

[12] The United Nations Security Council endorsed this new mission in its resolution 1088. For the implications of these additional duties on the IPTF's mission, see UNSC, *Report of the Secretary General pursuant to Security Council Resolution 1088 (1996)*, S/1997/224, 14 March 1997. Available on http://www/un.org

The international community also viewed economic reconstruction as essential for achieving a lasting peace. To that effect, the European Union (EU), the World Bank (WB), and the European Bank for Reconstruction and Development (EBRD) prepared a three-to-four-year, $5.1 billion Priority Reconstruction Plan designed to jump-start the local economy, help develop common government institutions, and create the conditions for a transition from socialist to market economy.

Lastly, in view of the complexity awaiting them in implementing the Dayton agreement, the parties requested the designation of a High Representative to facilitate their own efforts and to mobilize and coordinate the activities of the various international organizations involved in the DPA civilian implementation. In December 1995, former Swedish Prime Minister Carl Bildt was designated as the High Representative. In April 1997, he was replaced by Mr. Carlos Westendorp from Spain.

Overview of DPA Implementation

After 20 months of operations, the parties' compliance with the DPA goals remained low and inconsistent. From the start, the parties mainly complied with the military provisions of the agreement. They observed the cease-fire, respected the four-mile-wide Zone of Separation (ZOS) from each side of the Inter-Entity Boundary Line (IEBL), and agreed to the cantonment of their heavy weapons. They also allowed IFOR and then SFOR to monitor their weapons sites and troop movements.

Finally, the parties granted Freedom of Movement to IFOR and the international community operating in B-H. Such level of compliance was achieved early in the operation, remained high during the IFOR operation, and continued under SFOR.[13] However, as of fall 1997, the parties have not fully complied with the measures designed to achieve lasting security. First, although the three factions have completed the reduction of their forces to the agreed-upon level of a total 300,000, the OSCE-supervised arms reduction program has not been fully complied with, as the Bosnian Serbs have constantly underreported their heavy weapons holdings. Second, negotiations for establishing regional arms control balance in and around the Former Republic of Yugoslavia (FRY) have not begun. Aside from the DPA provisions, the United States is pursuing its own program intended for regional stabilization. Under the "equip and train program," the United States is unilaterally arming and training the Federation military. Officially, the goal of this program is to deter a Bosnian Serb aggression against the Bosniacs and Croats.[14] This program progressed at a slower pace than expected due to a lack of cooperation between the Bosnian Croats and Bosniacs.

---

[13] See Appendix 3 for the milestones in the implementation of annex 1A.

[14] This program caused recurring tensions between the United States and its European allies. European countries and NATO commanders have long argued that the equip and train program will provoke arms race and regional destabilization either by provoking a reaction from the Bosnian Serbs (who see the program as a threat) or by encouraging the Bosniacs and/or Bosnian Croats into attacking the Serbs or each other.

As for the civilian aspects of the DPA, progress has been slow and inconsistent. Although the parties regularly stated their commitment to the DPA full implementation, they have multiplied the stumbling blocks on the road to reconciliation, leading many observers to believe that "Dayton implementation is but continuation [of the war] by other means."[15]

National elections, intended as a first step in the development of Bosnia's democratic institutions, took place on 14 September 1996. However, the OSCE (who organized and supervised the process) concluded that the elections had not been fully free and fair.[16] The High Representative (along with Western governments) considered the elections as a necessary first step. Carl Bildt explained that

> the elections were absolutely necessary in order to bring us into the fourth and decisive phase of implementation of the Peace Agreement this year—the setting up of the common institutions. Without setting up these institutions, the country would remain partitioned in every reasonable sense, with the military IFOR command and the Office of the High Representative being the only

---

[15] Ivo Daalder, "Three Choices in Bosnia," *The Washington Post*, 18 July 1997, p. 21.

[16] The OSCE coordinator for international monitoring reported that the ability of all Bosnian political parties to campaign in a free and fair atmosphere, receive equal treatment before the law, and obtain equal access to the media was *below the minimum OSCE standard*. During the national elections campaign, the three dominant parties (the HDZ in the Croat area of the Federation, the SDA in the Bosniac-held territory, and the SDS in Republika Srpska) harassed and intimidated opposition political parties, while they tightly controlled the media and used them to promote fear and prejudice in the electorate. See U.S. General Accounting Office, *Bosnia Peace Operation: Progress Toward Achieving the Dayton Agreement's Goals*, GAO/NSIAD-97-132, Washington, D.C., May 1997, p. 8.

existing nationwide structures. Without these elections, the country was bound to develop into a new Cyprus.[17]

However, other organizations dispute that assessment because the elections legitimized the political parties and leaders who engineered the war, carried out widespread ethnic cleansing, and did not fully accept the principle of a unified, democratic, and multi-ethnic Bosnia. These organizations thus considered the elections as a setback in the process of recreating a democratic and multi-ethnic Bosnia.

Indeed, the elections should have paved the way for forming the institutions envisioned at Dayton. However, disagreements over the DPA requirements and over the scope and authority of the national institutions slowed the process. According to the High Representative, Carlos Westendorp, "little is achieved without prompting by, or support from my office as lack of political will to cooperate constructively, the danger of the renewal of confrontation mentality, mutual distrust and accusations continue to stall the peace process."[18] (See table 1: Progress achieved in creating national institutions, as of September 1997.) There were three major obstacles in building national institutions:

---

[17] Carl Bildt, "The Prospects for Bosnia," *RUSI Journal*, December 1996, p. 2.

[18] UN Secretary General, *Report for the High Representative for Implementation of the Peace Agreement on Bosnia and Herzegovina to the Secretary General*, S/1997/542, 11 July 1997. Available on http://www.un.org

- "The main barrier to political implementation is minority fear. Serbs and Croats are afraid as minorities in Bosnia; Muslims are afraid as a minority in the region. This fear bolsters extremists in all three communities."[19]

- The Bosniacs and Bosnian Croats made limited progress in establishing the Federation institutions. As of fall 1997, few common institutions existed and those that did were barely functioning. Observers still considered that real power remained in separate entities.[20]

- The Bosnian Serb leaders of Republika Srpska sought a weak central government, while the Bosniacs wanted a strong central government. For example, in summer 1997, the High Representative expressed concern at the RS national assembly adopting legislation not in accordance with the Bosnia-Herzegovina constitution. His efforts to bring the RS legislation in conformity with the B-H constitution had not succeeded as of July 1997.[21]

---

[19] David Last, *Implementing the Dayton Accords: The Challenges of Inter-Agency Coordination,* paper presented for Cornwallis II: Analysis of Conflict Resolution, held at the Pearson Peacekeeping Center, Cornwallis Park, 8-10 April 1997, p. 10. This sentiment is echoed by Susan Woodward, "The General Framework Agreement for Peace (GFAP) signed at Dayton and Paris is only a cease-fire. [The parties] do not accept the accord as definitive politically, seeing it only as an insecure stepping-stone. Each is still fighting the war for statehood," in "Bosnia," *The Brookings Review,* Spring 1997, vol. 15, no 2, p. 29.

[20] According to a General Accounting Office study, 16 months after the DPA, real government power in the Federation continued to reside in separate Bosniac and Croat government structures. For example, as of May 1997 (when the study was released), the two parties had not agreed on a municipality law. In another startling example, the European Union (EU) efforts to reunify the (symbolic) city of Mostar had not succeeded. See U.S. General Accounting Office, *Bosnia Peace Operation: Progress Toward Achieving the Dayton Agreement's Goals*, GAO/NSIAD-97-132, Washington, D.C., May 1997, p 46.

[21] UN Secretary General, *Report from the High Representative for Implementation of the Peace Agreement Bosnia and Herzegovina to the Secretary General, S/1997/542,* 11 July 1997. Available on http://www.un.org

Table 1: Progress Achieved in Creating National Institutions, as of September 1997 [22]

Institution	Function under Dayton	Status as of September 1997
Presidency	Executive body of the national government.	Meets regularly with representatives from all ethnic groups to establish national, multi-ethnic institutions. Reached several agreements.
Council of Ministers	Implements policies and decisions of national government.	Meets regularly since January 1997. Considers numerous matters with no discernible results. Ministries still have no staff, no funding, no office space, no effective authority.
Parliamentary Assembly	Enacts national legislation to implement Presidency decisions, approves national budget, ratifies treaties.	Met three times and passed little legislation (most notably the quick-start package).
Standing committee on military matters	Coordinates military matters at national level.	Inaugural session in July 1997. No significant decision.
Constitutional court	Highest appellate court. Resolves disputes over constitution and between entities.	Nine judges appointed. Constitutive session in May. Drafts procedures under OHR auspices.
Central Bank	Issues currency and conducts monetary policy.	Agreed on single currency, but different currencies in use in each party's territory. The German Mark is the only nationwide currency.

---

[22] This table is extracted from U.S. General Accounting Office, *Bosnia Peace Operation: Progress Toward Achieving the Dayton Agreement's Goals*, GAO/NSIAD-97-132, Washington, DC, May 1997, p 45. The original table was updated to reflect the changes post-March 1997.

In spite of multiple commitments from the parties to facilitate returns, refugees have not returned to Bosnia at the rate expected by the international community or wished by the asylum countries.[23] To date, less than 300,000 displaced persons and refugees (out of two million) have resettled in B-H. Most of these are majority returns.[24] Despite the UNHCR's efforts to plan for massive returns (as outlined in the "Repatriation and Return Operation 1997"), these have not happened. In fact, many factors act as powerful disincentives to returns: lack of security for returnees, administrative obstacles (most notably the limited ability to reclaim property), destruction (of housing, transport, or basic infrastructure), and poor economic prospects (absence of jobs). But more importantly, the three parties have not delivered on their promise to help refugees return. Through political maneuvering and outright violence, all three parties have consistently prevented minority returns, for example, Bosniacs returning to settle in Republika Srpska or Bosnian Serbs returning to Bosniac-held territory. The Bosnian Serbs have repeatedly stated that they can not allow Bosnian Croats and Bosniacs to resettle in Republika Srpska. Bosnian Croats have prevented Bosnian Serbs from resettling in the western part of the Federation. Bosniac authorities have opposed minority returns in Sarajevo and

---

[23] See for example, William Drozdiak, "Germany Escalates Drive to Repatriate Bosnians," *The Washington Post*, 3 April 1997, p. 28.

[24] The term "majority return" designates the return of refugees of one ethnic group into areas majoritarily populated (and thus politically dominated) by the same ethnic group. It is opposed to "minority returns" whereby refugees of one ethnic group resettle in areas dominated by another ethnic group.

Bugojno.[25]   In addition, international observers and IFOR/SFOR officials believe the Bosniac authorities have used DPREs' attempted returns in areas controlled by another entity to re-occupy strategically important areas, mainly within Republika Srpska. In response, the international community established an "open city program" whereby the UNHCR offered support and material assistance to villages and municipalities that welcomed residents from all ethnic communities.

Widespread returns were even more difficult as freedom of movement across entities did not exist for the local population. Indeed, police forces throughout the country routinely stopped vehicles bearing plates from other entities and harassed their occupants. These widespread practices actually "prevent the population from exercising its right to move freely around the country."[26] The international community tried to counter these practices. The UNHCR ran inter-boundary lines buses which allowed people from one ethic area to visit family or sites in an area controlled by another ethnic group. In May 1997, the IPTF and SFOR introduced a more aggressive checkpoint policy whereby all static police checkpoints in place for more than 30 minutes without

---

[25] See U.S. General Accounting Office, *Bosnia Peace Operation: Progress Toward Achieving the Dayton Agreement's Goal*, GAO/NSIAD-97-132, Washington, D.C., May 1997, p. 45. As a result of the parties' lack of enthusiasm for minority returns, the international community has registered few successes in this realm. For example, in Spring 1997, 1,000 Bosniacs managed to resettle in Banja-Luka (Republika Srpska). However, such happenstance were rare and almost limited to large cities. In rural areas, minority returns are virtually non-existent.

[26] UN Secretary General, *Report of the Secretary-General on the United Nations Mission in Bosnia and Herzegovina*, S/1997/468, 16 June 1997, p. 2. Available on http://www.un.org

explicit authorization from the IPTF were to be removed. Despite these efforts, freedom of movement for non-international persons was still limited.

Reconstruction is underway. The $5.1 billion Priority Reconstruction Program approved in 1996 was designed to (1) finance emergency reconstruction projects and (2) promote sustainable economic development by financing small businesses and encouraging foreign investment in Bosnia-Herzegovina. The international community's effort benefited Bosnia. Some infrastructure and basic services were restored and small-sized business loans helped revive commerce. According to a November 1996 donor report, economic conditions slightly improved, especially in the Federation.[27] However, the parties' limited cooperation slowed down the reconstruction process. For example, in 1996, the RS only obtained 2 percent of the reconstruction pledges in response to its lack of cooperation. In 1997, the OHR postponed the donor's conferences several times due to lack of parties' cooperation.[28] The repeated postponements thus delayed the reconstruction efforts.

Finally, democratization of institutions and minds proved a difficult process. The restructuring of police forces and judicial systems into democratic institutions did not

[27] For example, unemployment has gone down from 90% to about 60%. The World Bank estimated that 250,000 jobs were created at the peak of the 1996 reconstruction program. Industrial production has risen to 20% of its pre-war level in the Bosniac-controlled area and to 85% of its pre-war levels in the Croat part of the Federation (this part of the territory was far less affected by the war). Income per capita, although extremely low, rose during 1996.

[28] See "IMF, global donors press Bosnia on reforms," *Journal of Commerce*, 6 March 1997, p. 3.

occur. The IPTF training program affected only a minority of officers in the Federation and (as of July 1997) had not begun in the RS. Moreover, throughout a series of incidents, police forces displayed little professionalism, as well as lack of respect for democratic principles. According to several watchdogs in B-H, police forces were involved in harassment, intimidation, and black-marketeering. They acted as a tool of repression. The reform of the judicial system did not seem to have left the starting block. Likewise, democratization of the media in Bosnia-Herzegovina is slow. Most media across the country remained under tight control of the dominating factions and carried the messages that fit their political masters. To date, the OHR and OSCE democratization and reconciliation efforts have produced few results.

By and large, after 20 months of international involvement, the political and cultural differences that sparked the war were not resolved and the parties showed little will to resolve them. At the Peace Implementation Conference held in Bonn, Germany, in early December 1997, the High Representative, Carlos Westendorp, acknowledged numerous problems, most notably the failure to organize the return of refugees and displaced persons; and the lack of human rights protections, laws on foreign investments, custom rules, national political parties, and public corporations. Faced with this reality, the DPA sponsors (France, Germany, Russia, United Kingdom, and United States) empowered the High Representative to impose binding decisions to overcome the parties' obstructionism and speed up the rebuilding process. [29]

The NATO Mandate[30]

The United Nations Security Council Resolution 1031 (December 1995) mandated NATO to deploy an Implementation Force (IFOR) to Bosnia and Herzegovina "to help ensure compliance with the military provisions of the DPA."[31] Specifically, IFOR (then SFOR) was mandated to—

- ensure continued compliance with the cease-fire agreed upon by the Parties on 5 October 1995;
- ensure that the parties' forces are withdrawn from a Zone of Separation (ZOS) on either side of the Agreed Cease-Fire line, to be completed on 19 January 1996;
- ensure that transfer of territory between the two entities is completed by 3 February 1996;
- ensure the collection of heavy weapons into cantonment sites and barracks and the demobilization of remaining forces (to be completed by 18 April 1996);

---

[29] See Office of the High Representative, *Bonn Peace Implementation Conference 1997: Bosnia and Herzegovina 1998: Self-sustaining Structures, Conclusions,* Bonn, 10 December 1997. Available at http://www.ohr.int/docu/. See also, William Drozdiak, "Bosnians Told to Adhere to Peace Process," *The Washington Post,* 10 December 1997, p A24.

[30] For a detailed analysis of NATO's involvement in Former Yugoslavia, see Gregory L. Schulte, "Former Yugoslavia an the New NATO," *Survival: The IISS Quarterly,* 39/1, Spring 1997, pp. 19-42.

[31] GFAP, *Annex 1A: Agreement on the Military Aspects of the Peace Settlement,* article 1 (general provisions), para 1.

- authorize and supervise the selective marking of the Inter-Entity Boundary Line (IEBL) and ZOS, which mark the new delimitation between the Federation and the Republika Srpska;
- control the airspace over Bosnia-Herzegovina (including civilian air traffic);
- assist international organizations in their humanitarian missions;
- observe and prevent interference with the movement of civilian populations and respond appropriately to deliberate violence to life and persons; and
- monitor the clearing of minefields and obstacles.

Annex 1A granted NATO a wide degree of authority to achieve its mission and established as a principle that IFOR had full authority to enforce the parties' compliance with annex 1A. It states that—

> the parties understand and agree that the IFOR Commander shall have the authority, without interference of any party, to do all that the Commander judges necessary and proper, including the use of military force, to protect the IFOR and to carry out the responsibilities listed above in paragraphs 2, 3 and 4, and they shall comply in all respects with the IFOR requirements.[32]

As a consequence, the parties agreed that to carry out its responsibilities, NATO has unimpeded right to observe, monitor, and inspect any forces, facility, or ac-

---

[32] GFAP, *Annex 1A: Agreement on the Military Aspects of the Peace Settlement*, article IV, para 5.

tivity in B-H that it believes may have military capability. Refusal, interference, or denial by any party of this right "shall constitute a breach of this annex and the violating party shall be subject to military action by the IFOR, including the use of necessary force to ensure compliance with this annex."[33] In conformity with these provisions, NATO commanders resorted to force to enforce the parties' compliance with annex 1A of the agreement.

As the parties quickly complied with annex 1A of the agreement, NATO's mission focus shifted. Although NATO forces continued to ensure compliance with the military provisions of the DPA, commanders increasingly supported the international organizations operating in Bosnia-Herzegovina. This requirement led IFOR (then SFOR) to establish working relationships with the principal civilian organizations (such as OHR, IPTF, UNHCR, and OSCE) called on to facilitate the civilian implementation. First, IFOR/SFOR and the international organizations established communication links and exchanged information on a regular basis. Second, IFOR/SFOR assisted the international organizations in their missions by providing manpower and logistical support.

---

[33] In regard with the IFOR enforcement role, annex 1A stated: "All Parties understand and agree that they shall be subject to military action by the IFOR, including the use of necessary force to ensure compliance, for: failure to remove all their Forces and unauthorized weapons from the four (4) kilometer Agreed Cease-Fire Zone of Separation within thirty (30) days after the Transfer of Authority, failure to vacate and clear areas being transferred to another Entity within forty-five (45) days after the Transfer of Authority; deploying Forces within areas transferred from another Entity earlier than ninety (90) days after the Transfer of Authority or as determined by the IFOR Commander; failure to keep all Forces and unauthorized weapons outside the Inter-Entity Zone of Separation after this Zone is declared in effect by the IFOR; or violation of the cessation of hostilities as agreed to by the Parties in Article II, in GFAP, *Annex 1A: Agreement on the Military Aspects of the Peace Settlement*, article 4, para 4b.

For example, IFOR supported the OSCE efforts to prepare and run the national elections in September 1996, as did SFOR during the 1997 municipal elections. IFOR and SFOR supported the IPTF police station inspections across the country. However, international organizations argued that NATO support was too limited. UNMIBH, OHR, and UNHCR officials stressed that NATO's unwillingness to use force to enforce the parties' compliance with the civilian annexes of the Dayton Peace Agreement would soon stall the process.[34] The situation notably evolved in summer 1997, as SFOR agreed to step up pressure on the parties to comply with the civilian implementation.

The IFOR and SFOR Command and Control Structures

Operation Joint Endeavour was a NATO-led operation authorized by the UN Security Council Resolution 1031 and carried out under the political direction of the Alliance's North Atlantic Council (NAC), as stipulated in annex 1A of the Dayton Peace Agreement. Eager to

---

[34] UNMIBH, UNHCR, and OHR officials stressed this point during non-attribution interviews conducted in October 1996 and March-April 1997. However, their statements reflected public positions taken by the High Representative. "I am of the opinion that it is the responsibility of the parties to cooperate fully with ICTY, and that this responsibility should remain with them. But as the same time, the international community cannot step back from its responsibility after having had the Security Council setting up the Tribunal, and after having devoted considerably and justified political attention to the war crimes issue. Infantry battalions are not designed or trained for criminal investigations or other law enforcement activities. But the present IFOR policy of apprehending indicted persons if encountered, and if the tactical situation allows, is more a non-policy than a proper policy. We must look at ways of creating instruments which will be necessary in selected cases in order to ensure that the one faction or the other simply does not make a complete mockery of the international community," in Carl Bildt, "The Prospects for Bosnia," *RUSI Journal*, December 1996, pp. 4-5.

avoid the command problems that crippled the UN effort between 1991 and 1995, NATO insisted that IFOR have a unified command structure. On 20 December 1995, most of the forces assigned to IFOR were placed under the operational control (OPCON) of Supreme Allied Command Europe (SACEUR), General Joulwan, USA. The principle of unified command also applied to 17 of the 18 non-NATO countries (mostly members of the Partnership For Peace—PfP) who chose to participate in the IFOR operations. All non-NATO forces but Russia were incorporated into the unified command structure alongside NATO forces, under the command of the IFOR Commander and his multinational divisional commanders.

The principle of a unified command, however, was not universal and four principal exceptions occurred. First, national support elements (NSE) remained under national control. Second, about 12 of the NATO nations provided National Intelligence Cells (NICs) that also remained under national command and control. Within NATO, intelligence is a national prerogative. Third, Russia's participation in IFOR was subject to special arrangements agreed to between NATO and Russia as the Russian government refused to place its brigade under NATO command and control. The Russian contingent was thus directly subordinated to Col. General Leontiy Shevtsov, as General Joulwan's Russian deputy. In theater, the Russian Brigade was placed under the tactical control of the U.S.-led Multinational Division

(North).[35] Fourth, U.S. PSYOP forces (which formed the core of the PSYOP capability) were not placed under NATO operational control. All these exceptions to the principle of a unified command chain remained valid under SFOR operations (as of August 1997).

The AFSOUTH/IFOR Structure

In December 1995, AFSOUTH assumed theater command of IFOR operations, while continuing its normal duties. AFSOUTH theater organization comprised nine subordinate commands (see figure 1).

Four of these commands were standing AFSOUTH subordinate commands. COMAIRSOUTH had responsibility for air operations. COMNAVSOUTH was responsible for coordinating naval operations in the Adriatic Sea. COMSTRIKFORSOUTH was responsible for carrier-based operations. COMLANDSOUTH had responsibility for the rear communication zone.

In addition to the standing AFSOUTH subordinate commands, SACEUR assigned the ACE Rapid Reaction Corps (ARRC)—a multinational (although principally UK and German) corps-level organization available for crisis response—to CINCSOUTH as the land component command. In addition, four temporary structures were set up. A Command for Support (C-SPT) was established in Zagreb for logistical support (personnel move-

---

[35] NATO basic fact sheet no. 10, "NATO's Role in Bringing Peace to the Former Yugoslavia," March 1997. Available on http://www.nato.int

Figure 1: AFSOUTH/IFOR Command and Control Structure

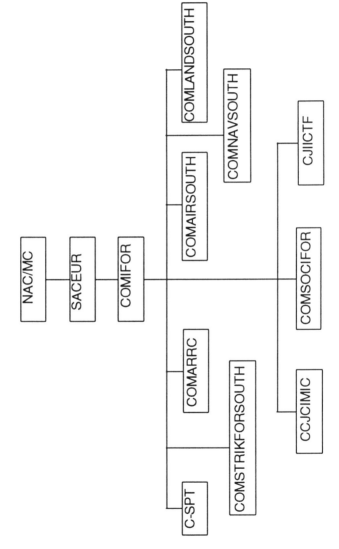

ments, contracting). A Special Operations Command IFOR (COMSOCIFOR) was also established, with U.S., UK, and French elements, to coordinate special forces operations in support of COMIFOR. A Combined Joint CIMIC (CJCIMIC) provided command and control for civil-military cooperation units throughout the theater of operations. Finally, the official organizational chart mentions a Combined Joint IFOR Information Campaign Task Force (CJIICTF), mainly composed of U.S. elements. In fact, the CJIICTF was not placed under NATO command and control, as U.S. DoD chose to retain control over U.S. PSYOP forces. This basic structure did not significantly change until November 1996 when LANDCENT assumed theater command.

Considering the nature of the operation (overwhelmingly a land operation), the ARRC played an important role until November 1996, and was the most prominent IFOR subordinate command. The ARRC had direct authority over three multinational divisions (MNDs): MND (SW), MND (SE), and MND (N). Each division was assigned an Area of Responsibility (AOR) to implement COMIFOR guidance.[36] However, the extensive overlap between IFOR and ARRC HQs geographic and issue areas of responsibilities (AORs) led to tensions, as the two staffs struggled throughout the year to define relative responsibilities.

---

[36] See Appendix 4 for a map of MNDs operations.

The LANDCENT/SFOR Command and Control Structure

The command and control structure changed in November 1996 when LANDCENT took over AFSOUTH/ARRC as the principal force component. The structure initiated then remained unchanged during SFOR operations.[37] COMLANDCENT assumed command of the new structure in early November 1996 (see figure 2).

The major changes with the previous command arrangements included the following:

- LANDCENT assumed AFSOUTH and ARRC responsibilities as the two headquarters were combined into one. The rationale for this reorganization was the desire to streamline the operation and alleviate the IFOR/ARRC HQs tensions. LANDCENT therefore assumed both theater-level and land component command responsibilities and COMLANDCENT had direct command authority over all land force components (with the exceptions noted above). The multinational divisions were placed under the responsibility of the Deputy Commander for Operations (DCOMOPS).
- The air and maritime components of the operation (COMSTRIKFORSOUTH, COMAIRSOUTH, and COMNAVSOUTH) were no longer subordinate, but supporting commands. As part of CINCSOUTH's command organization, they were not placed under COMSFOR's direct control.

---

[37] At least until this report went to print.

Figure 2: LANDCENT/SFOR C2

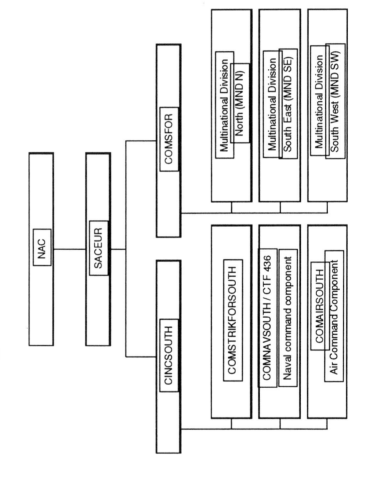

- As under AFSOUTH/ARRC arrangements, the Combined Joint Special Operations Task Force (CJSOTF) and the Combined Joint Information Campaign Task Force (CJICTF) remained under U.S. command and control. However, in the course of 1997, DoD agreed to place its PSYOP forces under NATO command and control, and in October 1997, PSYOP forces transferred to SACEUR C2.

Chapter 2:
The Public
Information Campaign

From early in the planning stage, NATO commanders expected information to play a critical role in the success of their operations in Bosnia-Herzegovina. As in any military endeavor, public support was central to mission accomplishment and Public Information (PI) was tasked with gaining and maintaining broad understanding for the mission. As in any peace operation, where force is only used as a last resort, public information was one of the "non-lethal weapons" at the commander's disposal to convince the parties and the populations to engage in friendly courses of action. According to Captain Van Dyke, USN, IFOR Chief Public Information Officer (CPIO), public information was "one of the elements of power used by the international community's political and military leaders to shape the operational environment, deter potential conflicts, and resolve crises in Bosnia-Herzegovina."[38]

---

[38] Capt. Mark Van Dyke, USN, IFOR Chief Public Information Officer, *Public Information in Peacekeeping: The IFOR Experience*, Briefing presented at NATO, Political-Military Steering Committee, Ad-hoc Group on Co-operation in Peacekeeping, NATO Headquarters, Brussels, 11 April 1997. Available at http://www.nato.int/ifor/afsouth

The importance given to public information in Bosnia-Herzegovina had far-reaching consequences for the structure and concept of operations. This chapter examines these requirements in detail.

Organization

Upon deployment, IFOR established a large PI organization (of about 90 persons) designed to provide extensive PI presence wherever significant military activity was taking place. To that effect, IFOR established PI offices and press centers throughout theater (see figure 3 for an organizational chart of IFOR PI).

IFOR and ARRC HQs PI offices and Coalition Press and Information Center (CPIC) were the principal elements of the PI structure. IFOR HQ PI directed the public information effort under guidance from NATO and SHAPE. ARRC PI was mainly responsible for PI issues relating to land operations in B-H. Both PI operations were situated in Sarajevo, where the centers of gravity of media and military activities were located. Major IFOR and international organization headquarters were established in Sarajevo. In addition, the international media presence was concentrated in Sarajevo.[39]

However, the recurring tensions between IFOR and ARRC HQs affected the PI operation. The tensions stemmed from a lack of clear delineation between the

---

[39] During the war, international reporters mostly remained in and around Sarajevo.

Figure 3: IFOR PI Organization

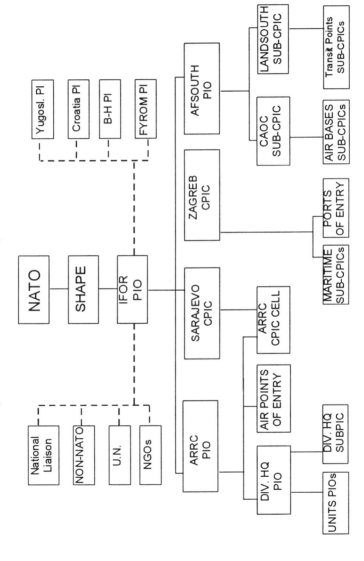

ARRC and IFOR HQs responsibilities. The tensions were especially visible at the Coalition Press and Information Center, a structure shared by IFOR and ARRC. Indeed throughout most of the IFOR operations, each headquarters sought to exercise a quasi-command relationship over the CPIC, mainly through their respective augmentees. This arrangement created tensions and complicated everyday operations.[40]

The structure was completed with PI offices and subordinate Coalition Press and Information Centers (sub-CPIC) established at divisional headquarters, where support activity was taking place, and at transit locations (most notably at port of entry and at arrival airports or airfields across B-H). The most important elements in that structure were the three MNDs PI offices and press centers (established in Tuzla, Banja Luka, and Sarajevo) as the divisions were likely to yield a considerable amount of media coverage. MNDs sub-CPICs were tasked with conducting day-to-day media activities, such as press releases, conferences, and media opportunities to promote IFOR activities.

Finally, IFOR HQ PI established a PI liaison officer (LNO) to the Joint Operations Center (JOC) to enhance the information flow between public information and the rest

---

[40] This situation resulted in several shortcomings. For example, both headquarters sometimes tasked the CPIC on the same topic at the same time, and both headquarters sometimes gave contradictory guidance to CPIC personnel. In the end, CPIC personnel seemed confused as to whom they were working for (IFOR HQ or ARRC HQ). The situation was further aggravated by the lack of continuity of leadership. The Sarajevo CPIC had 7 different Directors or acting Directors in 10 months (from Dec 95 to Oct 96), 2 of whom returned to their country before the end of their tours. This personnel turmoil made it difficult to enforce the chain of command. Despite several attempted fixes, the problem was only solved when LANDCENT assumed theater command in November 1996.

of the headquarters. The JOC LNO presence worked to mutual benefit. He provided a rapid link between the forces and the PIO, thus helping the PIO better anticipate incidents. He also aided the information flow in the other direction, as the PIO often learned of valuable information that the LNO could pass to the JOC.

LANDCENT/SFOR Changes

The PI structure changed in November 1996, when LANDCENT assumed responsibility from AFSOUTH/ARRC in Sarajevo and after the transition from IFOR to SFOR in December 1996. The most significant changes included the following elements:

- The AFSOUTH-to-LANDCENT transition generated some organizational changes at headquarters level as two headquarters (IFOR and ARRC) collapsed into one (LANDCENT). As a result, the Sarajevo CPIC supported only one headquarters rather than two.
- Further changes resulted from the reduction of forces subsequent to the transition from IFOR to SFOR (20 December 1996). With 34,000 troops in theater (against more than 60,000 for IFOR), the SFOR PI organization was reduced. Subsequently, several subordinate-CPICs were closed, such as Ploce.
- Finally, after the municipal elections took place (September 1997), SFOR HQ moved the press center from the Holiday Inn to the Tito Barracks.

Concept of Operation

To effectively reach its target audiences, IFOR's message first needed to convince the reporters, who mediate the information. To convince reporters, IFOR PI needed to establish credibility. To be credible, IFOR PI needed to "tell the story as it is," to make as much information as possible easily available and to be ready to answer (as candidly as possible) reporters' questions. To ensure that its message be heard, IFOR adopted a proactive posture designed to stimulate media interest in its operations. The PI strategy was thus based on three principles: a proactive public information policy; a free and open media access policy; and complete, accurate, and timely reporting. This section examines the pillars of IFOR's public information policy and its implication on the command and control structure.

A Proactive Information Policy

As negotiations closed down in Dayton and the likelihood of a NATO deployment increased, media interest in the Bosnia story grew anew. Under increasing media pressure, NATO established a proactive public information policy designed to promote IFOR's role and achievements by stimulating media and public interest in IFOR activities and operations. A proactive public information policy "dictates that attempts will be made to stimulate media and public interest about an issue or activity for the purpose of informing the public."[41] The

---

[41] SHAPE, "Annex A: Public Information Terms and Definitions," *ACE Directive 95-1: ACE Public Information Operations,* NATO UNCLASSIFIED, Mons, August 1995, p A-1.

policy consisted of regular (and numerous) media opportunities including daily press conferences, regular press releases, making commanders available for interviews, and media activities (such as going on patrol or following the activities of a civil affairs officer). Through this proactive policy, NATO sought to set the media's agenda on operations in Bosnia and to get its message across through multiple venues and occasions.

The proactive policy was critical early in the operation, as NATO needed to dissociate itself from the ill-fated UNPROFOR mission. To that effect, IFOR PI released detailed information about IFOR operations and encouraged the media to cover IFOR activities. NATO seized the opportunity of renewed interest in the Bosnia story to send a clear message to the factions that IFOR troops were well-led, well-trained, well-equipped, and ready to respond to any challenge through the use of force if necessary.

Although media interest shifted rapidly toward the civilian aspects of the Dayton implementation, the proactive policy remained a centerpiece of IFOR PI activities throughout *Operation Joint Endeavour*. IFOR maintained daily press conferences, released regular press releases, kept in close contact with the press corps, and continued to organize numerous media opportunities covering the wide range of IFOR activities in B-H. For example, opportunities to follow units on patrols, or to cover de-mining or civil affairs activities, or to stay with units in the field were made available to international and local reporters. In addition, IFOR publicized its activities in support of international organizations. For example, throughout the summer of 1996, IFOR PI advertised IFOR support to the OSCE in the preparation and execution of the national elections.

With the transition to SFOR, the PI policy became less proactive. SFOR PI, anticipating a NATO withdrawal from B-H in June 1998, downplayed SFOR activities and role and encouraged the civilian organizations to take the relay.[42] SFOR continued to participate in regular activities (most notably the daily press briefing, then held five times a week). However, SFOR PI public posture focused on its "military" activities such as patrols, weapon site inspections, or de-mining activities. SFOR PI no longer advertised large sectors of its activities, such as civil-military cooperation and support to the international organizations. For example, during IFOR, CIMIC fact sheets and photographic material on civil affairs teams' reconstruction efforts were on display at the CPIC. SFOR ended these practices, on the ground that "we don't do nation-building."[43]

A Free and Open Media Access Policy

Conditions within Bosnia-Herzegovina dictated that IFOR adopt a free and open press access policy whereby journalists could move freely around the the-

---

[42] This conclusion stemmed from conversations with SFOR PI staff, including Col. Rausch, USA, SFOR Chief Public Information Officer; Col. Baptiste, FRA, Deputy Chief Public Information Officer; LTC Hoehne, USA, Acting CPIC-director; and Maj. White, CA, SFOR spokesman. All interviews took place in Sarajevo during March-April 1997.

[43] Interview with LTC Hoehne, USA, acting CPIC director, Sarajevo, March 1997.

ater of operation. Throughout the war, journalists had access to the territory of Bosnia-Herzegovina. Transportation to and from B-H was available and local authorities did not systematically prevent journalists from traveling to and from the country. However, although possible, traveling to Bosnia remained a dangerous activity throughout the war.[44] The October 1995 cease-fire restored conditions for relatively safe travel across the country. The policy adopted in December 1995 was still in use at the time of writing.

According to this policy, journalists were allowed to move freely around the theater of operations. IFOR required that all journalists seeking access to military elements be registered with NATO. This was an easy process for any journalist working for an established media outlet, who was registered and issued a theater-access badge. This badge allowed reporters to go freely in and around the country and to enter IFOR compounds. In addition, under certain conditions, journalists could benefit from military equipment, such as transportation (mainly inside theater) or communications. However, reporters were expected to provide for their own accommodations and food.

This policy resulted in two major benefits. First, it contributed to IFOR's efforts to establish and maintain good relations and a high level of credibility with the media— especially with the American media. Considering that all restrictions placed on reporters during several op-

---

[44] Forty-five journalists were killed covering the Bosnian war between April 1992 and December 1995.

erations during the 1980s and 1990s strained military-media relations, adopting a liberal policy would score high with the journalists covering the Bosnia story.[45] Second, adopting the free and open access policy freed the IFOR PI from a substantial logistical burden. Indeed, IFOR did not have to worry about providing transport, accommodations, or food for the incoming journalists.

Complete, Accurate, and Timely Reporting

During planning, CINCSOUTH Admiral Smith, USN, established the need to gain and maintain a high level of credibility with the media as a prerequisite for gaining the public's support and confidence for the mission. Providing IFOR's target audiences (the international and local media, the local population, and to a lesser extent the Former Warring Factions) with "complete, accurate, and timely information" was the key element of this policy. According to Capt. Van Dyke, USN, IFOR chief PIO, Admiral Smith felt that in an open and transparent operation such as IFOR, "if we [IFOR] know, they [the media] know."[46] Under such circumstances, disseminating relevant information—including bad news and mistakes—as quickly as possible was essential. It would help the command establish good relations with the

---

[45] For an overview of the military restrictions on media access to the battlefield, see Pascale Combelles Siegel, *The Troubled Path to the Pentagon's Rules on Media Access to the Battlefield,* U.S. Army War College, Strategic Studies Institute, May 1996.

[46] Interview with Capt. Van Dyke, USN, IFOR chief PIO, Sarajevo, 17 October 1996.

press, and promote broad understanding of the mission. Timely and accurate reporting were essential elements of IFOR's proactive PI policy.

Implications of PI Concept of Operation on C2

The IFOR PI strategy had important command and control implications. To provide complete, accurate, and timely information to the media, PI needed rapid information flow and thus had to be closely tied into operations. Specifically, PI needed to have close association with their commanders (to be kept abreast of their thinking), to be kept informed of plans and of operations and incidents as they unfolded (or as close as possible to that), and to be allowed to release information quickly to the press.

Commander Support

Following plans, most commanders gave full support to their PI teams and established close relations with their PIOs. For example, Admiral Lopez, USN, COMIFOR during summer and fall 1996, held his first and last daily meeting with Capt. Van Dyke, USN, the IFOR Chief PIO, or his deputy. COMARRC, LtGen Walker, UKA, usually chaired the daily ARRC information coordination group where information activities were considered. Both ARRC and IFOR CPIOs enjoyed an open-door policy with their commanders and had one-on-one informal meetings as the situation dictated. This close relationship allowed the PIOs to gain insights into the commanders' thinking and wishes. It also ensured that the commander knew what was developing in the news media. Such a close relationship between the commander and the PI is all the more remarkable as it seemed to be relatively unusual. As Capt. Van Dyke put it: "I had never enjoyed so close a relationship with my commander in my previous assignments. This was unusual, but it was a critical condition of our success."[47]

Such an open and close relationship, however, did not seem to continue under SFOR. The SFOR CPIO had more limited access to his commander than his IFOR predecessor. The following changes in the CPIO/ COMSFOR relationship occurred:

- The Chief PIO no longer enjoyed an open-door policy with his commander.
- COMSFOR no longer cultivated an informal relationship with his chief spokesman.
- Encounters between the CPIO and the COMSFOR were limited to formal morning meetings.

Relationship Between PI and Operational Staff Components

In addition, throughout the operation, commanders at IFOR and ARRC HQs ensured that the flow of information between PI and operations was adequate, allowing

---

[47] Interview with Capt. Van Dyke, USN, IFOR CPIO, Sarajevo, 17 October 1996.

PI to gain complete and timely knowledge of current and future operations, even when classified. The highest integration occurred at IFOR HQ level, where the PI office had a liaison officer (LNO) permanently assigned to the Joint Operations Center (JOC). The LNO, sitting next to the JOC director, assessed all information coming to the operations center and reported to the chief PIO or his deputy any situation that might become a news story. "My goal is to let the chief PIO be aware of what is going on and let him decide based on the facts what PI implication some events might have."[48] The JOC LNO also tracked down information published in press reports but where no operational information was (yet) available. His presence also benefited the JOC as he provided information gathered by the PIO to the operations center. The close proximity of the PI office and the JOC (almost literally next door to each other) facilitated the information flow between PI and operations.[49] However, the integration with CJ3 seemed to decline during SFOR operations. SFOR PI still had a representative in the JOC, but his office was not necessarily read into operational planning.

The situation was less integrated at subordinate headquarters and at division level. At ARRC, MND (N), and MND (SW) the PI offices did not have a full-time permanent liaison officer assigned to the operations room.

---

[48] Interview with Captain Feliu, USA, PI LNO to the JOC, Sarajevo, 11 October 1996.

[49] For example, IFOR Deputy Chief PIO went regularly to the operations center. Interview with Col. Serveille, FRA, IFOR DCPIO, Sarajevo, 27 October 1996.

In most cases, the pace of activities did not require a full-time liaison.[50] In addition, the ARRC, MND (N), and MND (SW) PI offices and operations room were not as conveniently located as they were at IFOR HQs level. For example, at both MNDs, the PI offices and operations room were located in different buildings. Casual walk-ins were therefore not easy. In these three headquarters, however, PIOs had free access to the operations room. MND (SE) was not as integrated.

Close integration was also ensured through IFOR and ARRC PIOs' attendance of various meetings and conferences. At headquarters level and at MND (N) and MND (SW), PIOs attended the commanders' staff meetings and the morning and evening conference calls. At MND (N)—

> Immediately behind Nash [USA, CG MND (N)] are two rows of staff officers. In wartime, the first row would be operational staff providing instant updates on fire support, air support, armor movements, intelligence and logistics. But this isn't war. Sitting behind Nash instead is a staff more familiar to a big-city mayor: a political advisor, an expert on civilian relations, representatives of two joint commissions, a public affairs specialist and a staff lawyer.[51]

---

[50] The ARRC, however, established a liaison in early September 1996 for monitoring information relating to the national elections. But according to the liaison officers, there was not enough work for them to do, except during the few days around the elections.

[51] Cited in Capt. Mark Van Dyke, USN, IFOR Chief Public Information Officer, *Public Information in Peacekeeping: The IFOR Experience*, Briefing presented at NATO, Political-Military Steering Committee, Ad-hoc Group on Co-operation in Peacekeeping, NATO Headquarters, Brussels, 11 April 1997. Available at http://www.nato.int/ifor/afsouth

By providing a knowledge of plans and a clear understanding of HQ policy and thinking, these arrangements enabled IFOR PI to anticipate and prepare for incidents and difficult issues. They provided a rapid link between PI and operations, thus minimizing the likelihood that a reporter would break a story about NATO operations that PIOs were not aware of, and, thus, prepared for.

The Information Chain

The arrangements were likely to be tested when a sudden incident would occur and be reported in the media before IFOR was prepared to make a public statement. To avoid these situations, PI needed to be aware of operations and incidents as they unfolded (or as close to this as possible). This, however, constitutes a tough challenge (see figure 4). Reporting through a chain of command is time-consuming, as each authority level processes information before reporting to higher headquarters. It is an even more time-consuming process in a multinational operation where each layer might speak a different language, translate the incoming report, and process it in its own language before passing it up. Such a lengthy process cannot adequately support the PIO needs for timely delivery of accurate information. A typical information flow up a military chain of command simply cannot compete successfully with media reporting.

The challenge stems from the inherent imbalance between a journalist's ability to report on the spot and the military's need to process information before it passes

Figure 4: Military Chain of Command vs. Journalistic Information Flow

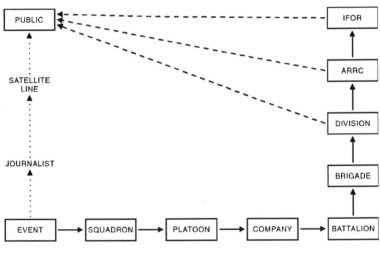

JOURNALIST'S FEED. POTENTIALLY INSTANTANEOUS.

it up the chain of command. First, journalists can relate any piece of news much faster than the military. Today's technology enables a journalist to broadcast an ongoing incident live (providing he or she is on the ground). While witnessing an incident, a journalist just needs to set up a satellite phone to break the news to his central offices. In a matter of minutes, the news may reach wide international audiences. By comparison, the military flow of information is much slower. Indeed, faced with the same incident, an officer will report the situation to his immediate higher headquarters. The process will be repeated until the information reaches a high enough level headquarters where the information can be cleared for public release. Second, a journalist may be asked to provide his "analysis," his personal interpretation of the situation to the best of his knowledge at the time of release. Military reporting, however, typically focuses on facts rather than impressions. Thus reporting might be delayed as attempts are made to confirm or complete the facts. Finally, the pressure to scoop the competition can lead to a situation where "being first is better than being right." Typically, it results in reporters going on air because something is happening, although it is unclear what is happening. Being on air matters most. Military reporting, on the other hand, typically relies on collecting all the facts and verifying information before passing it up to higher headquarters. For the journalist, immediacy can override accuracy. For the military, accuracy can override immediacy.

This imbalance is dangerous because a higher head-quarters can learn about an operation or an incident from the TV news rather than from its subordinate head-quarters. The likely results are potentially important as higher headquarters often treat the media reporting as fully factual whether this is truly the case or not. In consequence, higher headquarters will often turn angrily to its subordinate elements for confirmation or explana-tions.[52] This type of intervention generates tensions between higher and subordinate headquarters and hurts the credibility and confidence necessary between lev-els of command. On occasions, the imbalance between military and journalistic information flow may affect de-cision making, either by producing a lasting impression on the decision maker or by his feeling forced to react in the heat of the moment.

IFOR's solution to this dilemma consisted of a vertical functional information chain linking all PIOs throughout theater. According to Colonel Serveille, IFOR deputy chief PIO, annex P to OPLAN 40105 explicitly autho-rized a direct liaison between public information organi-zations at all levels of IFOR operations.[53] The chain of information worked in coordination with the chain of command. Operational information was reported throughout the chain of command. Operational infor-

---

[52] This happened when during the U.S. intervention in Haiti (*Operation Uphold Democracy*, September 1994), Marines opened fire on local police who pulled their weapons at them in Cape Haitien, killing ten. Apparently, the Pentagon and the White House learned of the incident from CNN. Authorities in Washington then directly contacted the local Marine commander around the C2 chain for an explanation of events.

[53] Interview with Col. Serveille, FRA, IFOR DCPIO, Sarajevo, 27 October 1996. The principle of the information chain was retained in SFOR planning.

mation of potential media interest was reported to the PIO, who reported it to the upper PIO echelon. The information chain allowed PIOs to communicate and exchange information without having to pass through all the layers of the chain of command, thus speeding up the information flow. Figure 5 presents the command and information chains, using MND (SE) as an example. In case of a serious incident, the process was further decentralized. Division or headquarters dispatched a PIO to collect firsthand information and deal with the press on-the-scene. In other words, PIOs had the authority to speak with other PIOs without violating the chain of command. These provisions greatly reduced the amount of time necessary for PI to obtain operational information of potential media interest and allowed an information flow that could support timely and accurate reporting.

The NATO operations in Bosnia revealed the importance of a separate information chain. In several incidents, IFOR PIOs gained timely awareness of situations that required a public response, which allowed them to better respond to the situation.[54] However, the chain of information did not always prevent the media from scooping IFOR PIOs. For example, PIOs in MND (N)

---

[54] For example, during fall 1996, as U.S. military equipment (from the Train and Equip program) began arriving in Croatia, IFOR PIOs spotted European soldiers wearing IFOR badges around the cargoes. They immediately referred the information to IFOR Chief PIO for further action (as IFOR media line stated that NATO had nothing to do with the program). The PIO related the information to the operations center for further verification. It turned out that, in fact, the soldiers were not IFOR. IFOR acted to have the badges removed and the PIOs received appropriate guidance to answer journalists' questions on the issue. In another instance, the MND (SW) PIO became aware that an attempted DPRE return in Tito Drvar was underway. He sent down one of his officers to gather information and prepare a public statement.

Figure 5: The Information Chain Process

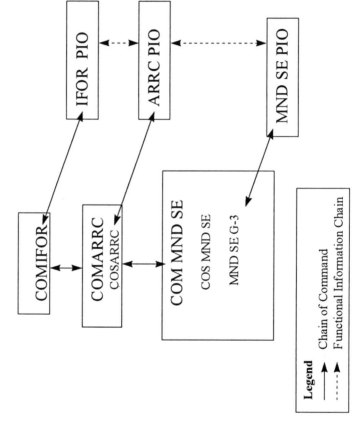

commented, although they did not provide specific examples, that journalists sometimes came asking confirmation of facts that they were completely unaware of.

No arrangement or procedure is fault-proof, and however integrated the PIO and operations are, incidents where the media will scoop the military will occur. This is all the more true in a peace support operation, where journalists move freely around the theater of operations. However, the consequences of these rare incidents can be either deflated or inflated by the higher command's reactions. Consequences are inflated or blown out of proportions when higher echelons impatiently require on-the-spot explanation. Consequences are minimized when higher echelons remember that the military chain is slower than media reporting and allow the subordinate headquarters to check the facts. The deflating process requires that higher commands have enough credibility with the media to delay releasing all information while asking the subordinate headquarters to check the matter. An information chain, however, is likely to decrease occurrences where the media scoops the PIOs. It is not a full-proof arrangement, but can be a valuable tool.

Delegation of Authority and Confidence Between Headquarters

The purpose of these arrangements would have been defeated if, in the end, PIOs were not allowed to release information to the media. Delegation of authority to a satisfactory level (i.e., a level that met PIO and journalist requirements) depended largely on the level of confidence between headquarters and principally be-tween NATO HQ, SHAPE in Belgium, and IFOR HQ in Sarajevo.

Establishing trust and confidence, especially between the strategic-level HQs in Belgium and the operational level (IFOR/SFOR HQ) was a challenge. During *Operation Deliberate Force*, AFSOUTH and NATO/SHAPE experienced difficult relations. NATO HQ and SHAPE requested to clear all public announcements, including all daily press briefings and releases of combat camera imagery.[55] Surprisingly, however, NATO, SHAPE, and AFSOUTH were able to dispose of *Deliberate Force's* legacy.

Under IFOR/SFOR, information release authority was delegated to the lowest possible level. COMIFOR/COMSFOR had authority to release (or to delegate release authority to appropriate levels) all theater-operational information. In addition, IFOR/SFOR PI were authorized to confirm news already obvious to the media without having to refer to higher headquarters. This provision greatly enhanced the PIs' ability to react quickly to fast-breaking news. Appropriate delegation of release authority allowed them to react in a timely fashion to fast-breaking news without interference from higher echelons. The higher the release authority is, the longer it can take to confirm and release relevant information.

---

[55] SHAPE requests caused recurring tensions with AFSOUTH PIOs and with journalists who openly wondered what "NATO was trying to hide." For a journalistic point of view on this issue, see Rick Atkinson, "NATO Tailors Bombing Information," *The Washington Post*, 16 September 1996, p 20.

In some cases, such delays can create tensions with the press and damage the military's credibility among journalists.

To make these arrangements work, confidence and trusting relationships were needed between NATO HQs and SHAPE; between SHAPE and IFOR/SFOR HQ; and between IFOR/SFOR HQ and its subordinate commands. This was mostly ensured through bureaucratic measures, by providing detailed guidance and situation reports (SITREPS), and by maintaining close contact throughout the PI structure. Throughout the operation, NATO and SHAPE exercised oversight of the PI operation through the production of Public Information Guidance (PIG). They provided all IFOR/SFOR PIOs with a general framework to keep events and incidents in theater in the broad political context and provided the Alliance's official position on the most important issues relating to the mission. When needed, further guidance was available directly from the NATO Secretary General's spokesman. IFOR/SFOR PI relayed this guidance to subordinate commands. Conversely, subordinate headquarters kept higher headquarters in SHAPE and NATO apprised of events in theater through a steady bottom-up information flow, including a daily telephone call to SHAPE PI for planning of the day's activities; production of a daily SITREP to SHAPE; production of a transcript of the daily press conference; and frequent interactions by telephone and e-mail. A similar stream of information went from SHAPE HQ to NATO HQ.

Public Information Activities

The PI strategy principles allowed IFOR and SFOR to provide a steady flow of information to journalists covering the operations. Aside from issuing guidance and producing SITREPS for higher and subordinate commands, IFOR and SFOR PI conducted the following activities:

- Everyday, IFOR/SFOR PI held a press briefing at 11.00 at the Sarajevo Holiday Inn. The briefing was the main venue by which the IFOR released information to the media and it typically focused on operations and events of the previous 24 hours. The daily briefing frequency was progressively downscaled from seven to five days a week when the tempo of operations calmed down.
- Special briefings were organized at the IFOR press center when needed, most notably during VIP visits.
- IFOR/SFOR PI maintained informal relations with journalists. Before and after the daily briefing, journalists, spokesmen, and public information officers gathered in the CPIC hallway around a cup of coffee for informal chats and interviews. The informal interactions allowed PIOs and journalists to gain insights into each other's work.
- IFOR/SFOR PI answered media queries. Any journalist could call the CPIC for information about operations. To that effect, the press center was open daily (except Sundays after the first few months of operations). In addition, a press officer was on duty 24 hours a day, 7 days a week to answer questions.

- IFOR/SFOR PI set up media opportunities for reporters and photographers. IFOR PI compiled regular lists of activities that reporters were welcome to attend. These proactive actions were curtailed substantially during SFOR operations.
- IFOR PI produced and made available illustrative material for journalists, such as photographs of IFOR activities and maps. It is unclear whether SFOR continued this practice.
- IFOR/SFOR PI notified the press of incidents and significant events through press releases.

Limiting Factors

Several factors limited the effectiveness of IFOR/SFOR public information operations. For example, as in any deployment, PIO faced shortages of equipment and communications. Such shortfalls, however, did not significantly limit the PIO's ability to conduct its mission.

The SFOR HQ progressively marginalized the CPIO and other PI staff roles within the command group. This decreased the PIO's contribution to mission accomplishment. The strong support the commander had given the PI did not seem to survive the turnover to LANDCENT. From then on, the CPIO interactions with the commander were limited primarily to formal morning meetings. More importantly, it also seems that the PI integration with other operational staffs (in particular the CJ3) decreased from AFSOUTH to LANDCENT. These changes decreased the PI's ability to effectively contribute to mission accomplishment. In a striking example, the CPIO learned of the raid to arrest two war criminals in Prijedor on 10 July 1997 only after it had already taken place. By this time, the Bosnian Serb media was already reporting events (with their interpretation of the events). This left the SFOR CPIO unable to assume a proactive posture but in a reactive mode with the "information" initiative in Serb hands.

But throughout the mission, the major limitation stemmed from the multinational nature of the operation. Creating a truly multinational PI apparatus was a challenge. The IFOR OPLAN called for a multinational PI apparatus centered around the establishment of multinational sub-CPICs led by an officer of the largest contributing nation in a given sector. This structure, however, did not materialize. For example, while MND (N) established a sub-CPIC, it was placed subordinate to a U.S. Joint Information Bureau (JIB).[56] The sub-CPIC did not have U.S. personnel, and the JIB only had Americans. The sub-CPIC represented the non-U.S. contingents serving in MND (N), while the JIB handled all matters relating to the U.S. forces. Throughout IFOR operations, the JIB directed all public information activities throughout the division's AOR, while the underemployed sub-CPIC personnel was left with marginal duties. Most notably, the sub-CPIC personnel handled press registrations and ran errands away from the Task Force

---

[56] In a multi-service U.S. deployment, the Joint Information Bureau is the press center and typically has representatives of several services involved in the operation.

Eagle compound, a function the JIB personnel could not handle due to force protection rules.[57] The sub-CPIC was suppressed altogether during SFOR operations. Likewise, MND (SW) sub-CPIC was mostly composed of British personnel. Early in the IFOR operation, the division preferred to wait for UK reinforcements rather than accept NATO personnel. Throughout IFOR operations, only MND (SE) eventually managed to establish a truly multinational sub-CPIC. Each major contributing nation to the division had a representative in the PI office. All representatives participated in the PI daily operations and planning.

Two factors made it difficult to establish a truly multinational PI apparatus. IFOR divisions headquarters were not multinational but run by the leading contributing nation. The press office was one of the few multinational staff components. In addition, commanders preferred to bring their own national PI staffs to run their PI programs.

In addition, in a large coalition such as IFOR/SFOR, room existed for different PI concepts. These differences made it more difficult to run a concerted campaign. Although the PIOs in theater operated under NATO and SHAPE guidance, they also remained imbued with their own national doctrines and procedures.

---

[57] In MND (N), U.S. and non-U.S. troops were submitted to two sets of force protection rules. Americans were required to wear full combat gear and travel outside the compound in four-vehicle convoys. None of these restrictions applied to the non-U.S. personnel. Since the JIB personnel could not easily muster the four-vehicle convoy to travel will all journalist, the JIB director often asked CPIC personnel to escort reporters within the AOR.

Even the three major contributors (the U.S., the UK, and France) had different approaches to public information operations. Table 2 presents the main differences in the three major coalition partners' public information policies.[58]

National systems of operation were a source of recurring problems as different PI doctrines and procedures led to misinterpretations, incomprehension, and difficulties among IFOR PI staff.[59] From observations in the field, it seemed that each PIO was working at least as much with his national doctrine as with OPLAN 40105, ACE directives, or NATO doctrine.[60] Problems regularly arose when PI staffs had to deal with incidents and unexpected events.

One set of problems arose from different views on the amount of information that should be released to the media. From observations in theater, it appeared that IFOR and ARRC HQs perspectives on this issue often conflicted. IFOR HQ policy, which was based on SHAPE

---

[58] Table 2 presents the principles guiding information policy in Bosnia-Herzegovina as reconstituted from public information doctrinal publications (when available) and from conversations with PI officers both in theater and in the various capitals concerned.

[59] This phenomenon was mostly documented for the IFOR period.

[60] For example, at MND(SW), PIOs used the UK MOD manual for public information officers to solve problems as they occurred. At MND(N), the JIB mainly worked with US doctrine and according to US procedures. The following is a concrete example of how PIOs sometimes reacted according to national rather than NATO principles. In October 1996, military photographers videotaped armed RS policemen beating up a journalist in the Zone Of Separation. The journalist asked for the tape to be released. At the IFOR PI morning meeting, a British officer argued that its release would be contrary to the 'green book' (UK MOD public information directives) instructions, whereas OPLAN 40105 authorized the release. Author's notes from IFOR HQ PI morning meeting, 16 October 1996.

Table 2: Major Contributors' Public Information Principles and their Implications

Country	Public Information Principles	Implications
U.S.	Public information is a command function. It is an operational tool. It is also a democratic requirement because people have a right to know. Publication of classified information by a journalist is not against the law.	Internal information and release of timely, complete and accurate information to the media. Requirements: (1) free and open policy (whenever feasible), (2) proactive policy and (3) easy access to commanders.
UK	Public information is an operational function (belongs to G3). Publication of operational information is forbidden by law and status.	Release of information should serve an operational purpose. Media don't have right of access to information. This is a granted privilege.
FR	Public information is a support activity. Media don't have a right of access to information.	Access to commander and operational information is inconsistent. Information policy is semi-active (a policy which seeks to information the media and public without intending to intensify media and public interest).

and U.S. public affairs principles, was clear: all information likely to be of interest to the media should be released unless precluded by troop safety and/or operational security. In addition, for the sake of credibility, IFOR HQ established the practice of confirming news already obvious to the media. Under no circumstances should an IFOR spokesman lie directly to a journalist as it may cause irreparable damage to his/her credibility. The ARRC HQ, however, did not fully adhere to these principles. On several occasions, IFOR HQ PI complained that ARRC PI officers were withholding information that the media would be interested in.[61] In addition, the ARRC seemed to strictly follow the British doctrine that one does not talk about ongoing or upcoming operations. For example, prior to the destruction of a large stock of ammunitions and explosives in Margetici, reporters noticed increased IFOR activity. Questioned by reporters at the daily briefing, the ARRC spokesman denied that anything was happening.[62] One could characterize the two headquarters' attitudes as follows: For IFOR, the question should always be: "Why should I not release the information?" For ARRC, the basic question seemed to be: "Why should I release this information?" The two concepts regularly generated conflict between the two headquarters.

---

[61] For example, early in IFOR operations, Gen. de la Presle's plane was hit by several rounds of fire during a landing at Sarajevo airport. The CPIC director, an ARRC augmentee, did not include in the press release that the plane had actually been hit. Interview with Col. de Noirmont, IFOR Deputy Chief Public Information Officer, Paris, 16 November 1996.

[62] Interview with Simon MacDowall, acting Sarajevo CPIC director during IFOR operations, Northwood, 17 February 1997.

There also were frictions between IFOR and subordinate headquarters about the level and type of information that should be reported up the chain of command/ chain of information. To be able to deliver complete, accurate, and timely information to the press, IFOR HQs PI expected fast, comprehensive, and accurate reporting from the subordinate commands. However, contingents did not always report as much information as IFOR felt it needed to handle media queries effectively. In some instances, contingents failed to report information that would reflect negatively on their attitudes or operations. In other cases, contingents failed to report on routine actions that they viewed as unimportant operationally. As a result, they did not report these "details" through the information chain. However, these details could have helped IFOR spokesmen deal with the media.[63]

Some contingents failed to closely associate their PI with their operational staffs. For example, at the French-led MND (SE), commanders seemed to consider the PI as a support activity. During the first months of the operation, PI did not have easy access to the operations room, did not attend the commander's conference calls, and were not associated with G2 or G3 activities. Things only improved slowly. Several months into operations, PIOs were tasked with presenting a daily press sum-

---

[63] On 9 January 1996, a Bosnian Serb sniper shot a woman on the Sarajevo tramway. The French immediately fired back at his position. At the daily briefing, the press accused IFOR of standing by and not doing anything. At first, IFOR PI could not counter those accusations because it was not aware of the French response. When they finally became aware of it, the issue was no longer of interest to the media and reported incorrectly internationally. Simon McDowall, Sarajevo CPIC director, spoke with the author, Northwood, 17 February 1997. (For an account of the incident, see Olivier Tramond, "Une mission inédite executée par le 3e RPIMa à Sarajevo : La création d'une zone de séparation en milieu urbain," *Les Cahiers de la Fondation pour les Etudes de Défense*, 6/1997, p. 53).

mary at the evening division conference call. By fall 1996, they gained unlimited access to the operations room. They then became more closely associated with operations as an organizational reform placed PI under G3 supervision in the fall of 1996. It seemed, however, that these reforms were too slow and incomplete to fully satisfy IFOR HQ PI.

Conclusion

The main concepts of IFOR/SFOR PI operations served the commander's needs and the public well. By providing complete, accurate, and timely information, IFOR/SFOR established credibility with the international media. Especially during IFOR operations, several internal arrangements supported the PI's ability to provide this information. These arrangements included a functional chain of information, close relationship between the PIO and commander, and delegation of release authority. However, multinationality sometimes limited a fully effective implementation of these principles. Moreover, these principles were better attuned to the international media than to the local ones. This gap meant that the psychological operations campaign, specifically targeted at convincing the local populations, was all the more important.

Chapter 3: Psychological Operations

NATO planners established the need for a campaign targeted at the local population of B-H and designed to shape attitudes and behavior in favor of IFOR (later SFOR) troops and operations. To carry out this task, IFOR's primary tool was its psychological operations campaign, called the IFOR Information Campaign (IIC).[64] Although an official NATO term, the term "psychological operations" was not used. Some NAC members did not want to be associated with a "psychological operations campaign." "IFOR Information Campaign" seemed to ease these fears.[65] However, there is little doubt that the "information campaign" was a psychological operations campaign. It was conducted by PSYOP forces and according to NATO's draft peace support psychological activities doctrine.[66]

---

[64] With SFOR, it became the Information Campaign (IC).

[65] This terminology creates some confusion, as the ARRC also used the term information campaign to describe the combined and synchronized use of public information and psychological operations. To avoid confusion, I use the term psychological operations rather than information campaign to describe the PSYOP campaign.

[66] See NATO, "Annex J: Peace Support Psychological Activities," *Bi-MNC Directive for NATO Doctrine for Peace Support Operations*, PfP UNCLASSIFIED, Brussels, 11 December 1995.

Organization

A Combined Joint Task Force under CJ3 supervision was responsible for implementing the NATO psychological operations campaign.   Under IFOR, the task force was called the Combined Joint IFOR Information Campaign Task Force (CJIICTF). With SFOR operations (20 December 1996), the name changed to Combined Joint Information Campaign Task Force (CJICTF).[67] Both task forces were directed by a U.S. Army Reserve Colonel, and were mainly composed of U.S. personnel and assets with supporting elements from France, Germany, and the United Kingdom.[68]

The IFOR Structure

The Task Force featured centralized planning and management at headquarters level, and decentralized execution by subordinate elements from divisions down to battalions. Figure 6 provides an organizational chart of the IFOR PSYOP campaign.

---

[67] Initially, the SFOR task force was called Combined Joint SFOR Information Campaign Task Force (or CJSICTF). Due to the difficulty of using the acronym as a word and discomfort with the even shorter version SIC (for SFOR Information Campaign), SFOR was removed from the Task Force's name.

[68] Several other contributing nations conducted some form of psychological operations. For example, the Spanish and Italian contingents used PSYOP in support of their civil-military cooperation (CIMIC) operations. These activities, however, were relatively small in scale and nature and were not conducted in support or in coordination with the IFOR Combined Joint IFOR Information Campaign Task Force, which is the focus of this chapter.

Figure 6: IFOR Information Campaign Organization

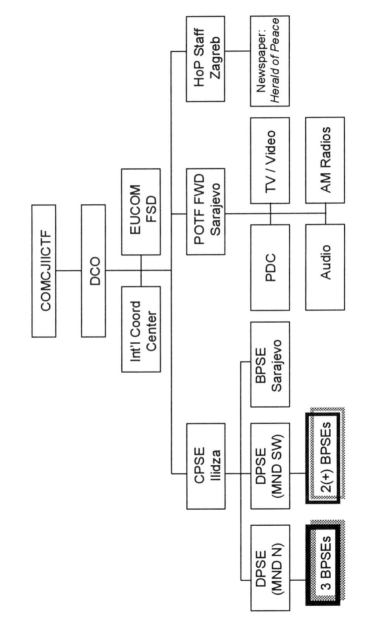

At the operational level, the CJIICTF had three elements:

- The headquarters was in charge of planning and managing the campaign.
- A PSYOP Task Force (POTF FWD) located in Sarajevo conceived and developed the products to be disseminated throughout theater and operated five IFOR radio stations.
- The HOP staff located in Zagreb produced the weekly newspaper called *The Herald of Peace*. After a few months of operations, the HOP staff joined the rest of the Headquarters in Sarajevo.

At the tactical level, support elements in charge of product dissemination were attached at corps, division, brigade, and battalion levels. PSYOP Support Elements (PSE) at division and brigade levels provided planning and execution expertise, while Tactical PSYOP Teams (TPTs) disseminated products and gathered feedback on the IIC effort.

The SFOR Structure

With the transition from IFOR to SFOR in December 1996, the PSYOP task force organization somewhat changed. Although the new CJICTF was still structured around a core U.S. element, the presence of foreign supporting elements increased notably. The significant changes to the IFOR organization included the following: (see figure 7 for an organizational chart):

Figure 7: SFOR Information Campaign Organization

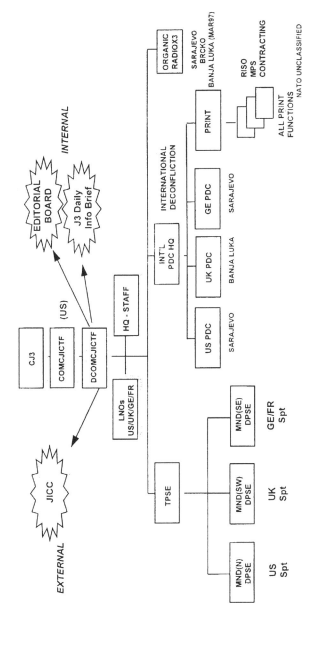

EXTERNAL

JICC

INTERNAL

EDITORIAL BOARD

J3 Daily Info Brief

CJ3

COMCJICTF

(US)

DCOMCJICTF

HQ - STAFF

LNOs US/UK/GE/FR

INTERNATIONAL DECONFLICTION

INT'L PDC HQ

US PDC
SARAJEVO

UK PDC
BANJA LUKA

GE PDC
SARAJEVO

PRINT

ALL PRINT FUNCTIONS

RISO
MPS
CONTRACTING

ORGANIC RADIO X3

SARAJEVO
BRCKO
BANJA LUKA (MAR97)

TPSE

MND(N) DPSE
US Spt

MND(SW) DPSE
UK Spt

MND(SE) DPSE
GE/FR Spt

NATO UNCLASSIFIED

- The headquarters and Product Development Cell (PDC) became multinational instead of all-U.S. France and the United Kingdom assigned liaison officers (LNOs) to the CJICTF headquarters. Both LNOs fully participated in the headquarters activities and provided liaison with the UK-led MND (SW) and French-led MND (SE). Finally, the CJICTF J3 supervised a Brigade PSYOP Support Element (BPSE) with three TPTs. The BPSE transported material to be disseminated to the divisions, carried out dissemination missions, and gathered feedback on the campaign's impact.
- U.S. PSYOP Support Elements (PSE) from division down to battalion levels only remained in MND (N). In the two other multinational divisions, U.S. PSE were replaced with troops from the contributing nations. In MND (SW), UK troops ran a tactical level campaign, creating and producing material relevant to the AOR. UK troops also disseminated the CJICTF products. In MND (SE), German and French troops operated in the GE and FR sectors (sometimes with the support of the BPSE based in Sarajevo).

Concept of Operations

The PSYOP campaign was designed to influence the local populations and FWF to cooperate with NATO activities. To achieve these goals, the task force ran a multimedia campaign, albeit a limited one, and sought to use step-by-step psychological processes to entice attitudinal changes.

A Multimedia Campaign

The PSYOP campaign sought to reach the local population through a multimedia campaign relying mostly on NATO-owned assets. In the Bosnia context, where the factions tightly controlled the local media and used them to propagate their self-serving propaganda, IFOR/SFOR needed to circumvent the local media to effectively reach the local audiences. Also, in a country where people are accustomed to modern media and have relatively sophisticated expectations, the PSYOP campaign sought to take advantage of several venues to disseminate its message. To achieve these goals, NATO resorted to a variety of self-owned media:

- A newspaper. IFOR printed a weekly newspaper, *The Herald Of Peace*. This publication became a monthly paper, *The Herald Of Progress,* with SFOR. In fall 1997, the CJICTF decided to only print special editions of *The Herald Of Progress.* The CJIICTF/CJICTF printed 100,000 copies of most of the first 65 issues published by fall 1997.
- A monthly youth magazine. The German OPINFO battalion developed *Mircko,* a monthly magazine designed to appeal to the teenage audience. Publication began in June 1996 and production has increased to reach 100,000 copies per edition in fall 1997.
- Radio stations. The number and location of the IFOR/SFOR radio stations varied throughout the operations. Originally, IFOR set up five radio stations located in the five most populated cities across the country: Sarajevo, Tuzla, Banja-Luka, Mrkonjic Grad, and Mostar (struck down by a lightning on 14 September

1996). During the first six months of SFOR operations, the CJICTF operated three radio stations in Sarajevo (Radio Mir), Brcko, and Coralici. In the fall of 1997, the French-led MND (SE) agreed to man and operate a new station in Mostar. These radio operated at least 18 hours a day with music, news bulletins, and messages.

- Television spots. As of March 1997, IFOR/SFOR had produced 51 television spots to be given to local stations throughout theater.
- Posters and handbills. More than 3 million posters and handbills were disseminated throughout theater between December 1995 and November 1997.

A Limited Campaign

The PSYOP task force was to abide by a number of limitations. First, the PSYOP task force was only allowed to run a limited campaign that relied on true and factual information. Second, the task force was under an obligation to always identify itself as the source of the information. It was forbidden to use disinformation or deception. Disinformation (also called grey propaganda) consists of disseminating information without specifically identifying any source, thus letting the target audience draw his or her own conclusions as to who put out the information. Deception (also called black propaganda) consists of disseminating information while letting the target audience believe it emanates from a source other than the true one.[69]

---

[69] North Atlantic Military Committee, "Annex A: Glossary of Psychological Operations Terms and Definitions," *MC 402: NATO Psychological Operations Policy*, NATO UNCLASSIFIED, Brussels, April 1997, p A-2.

Third, the nature of this peace support operation also limited the nature of the message. Unlike in wartime, there were no declared enemies in B-H. Therefore, messages undermining the factions (legitimately elected in September 1996) were deemed inappropriate, even though the factions regularly stalled or prevented full implementation of the agreement they had signed. For example, the CJICTF could remind people that all parties supported the right of refugees to return. It could also praise multi-ethnicity or give examples of reconciliation processes. However, it could not tell the people of Bosnia that their leaders did not live up to their promises.

A Step-by-Step Psychological Process

Within these constraints, the PSYOP task force sought to use psychological processes to achieve attitudinal changes. According to Colonel Schoenhaus, commander of the (SFOR) CJICTF, the campaign "chose to expose the local populations to deliberate sequences of ideas selected for their potential psychological impact in a step-by-step process to create in the mind of the target audience an acceptable alternative course of action."[70]

This process involved carefully selecting the messages. The CJIICTF had the latitude to select the facts it chose to release as it was not compelled to "tell the truth, the whole truth, and nothing but the truth." It therefore chose which and how much information to put forward, and

---

[70] Col. Schoenhaus, USAR, COMCJICTF from December 1996 to August 1997, interview with the author, Sarajevo, CJICTF Headquarters, 27 March 1997.

how to argue its case. For example, an explanatory pamphlet on the Brcko arbitration decision released in March 1997 throughout Republika Srpska did not mention that the RS leadership had rejected the decision. In another example, the SFOR chief information officer insisted that a *Herald Of Peace* article on education should not quote a Bosnian Croat Minister explaining that children in territory under Croatian military control would be taught the Croatian version of Bosnia's history. The Chief Information Officer later explained that the PSYOP campaign was not in the business of informing, but in the business of convincing. Thus, because the Bosnian Croat Minister's declaration contradicted the DPA objectives of rebuilding a democratic and multi-ethnic Bosnia, it should not be reported in *The Herald Of Peace*.

In addition, the PSYOP task force presented messages in a specific sequence to obtain a cumulative effect leading to a change in attitude. For example, in support of voter registration for the national elections, the PSYOP task force first released products showing the benefits of democracy and voting. After the awareness phase, the task force moved to encouraging the voters to register for the particular election.

Alteration to the Original Concept

The original concept of operation, described above, did not change much over the course of both IFOR and SFOR operations. Throughout, the campaign remained under the same limitations and sought to use step-by-step psychological processes to entice attitudinal change. The only major change resulted from the perceived lack of readership.[71] Although IFOR products were widely available throughout Bosnia-Herzegovina, the CJIICTF felt it did not reach the desired level of readership. Early in the IFOR operation, the CJIICTF only resorted to IFOR-owned media to disseminate its products. Tactical teams roamed Bosnia-Herzegovina to distribute *The Herald Of Peace* and *Mircko*, and to disseminate posters, handbills, and pamphlets. Meanwhile, the headquarters set up five radio stations in the most populated cities of the country and progressively increased the programming to 18 hours a day.

Throughout the operations, IFOR and SFOR PSYOP campaigns were not adapted to the local populations' media consumption habits.[72] The PSYOP campaigns relied primarily on printed material (newspaper, news magazines, and posters), while the Bosnians' preferred medium was television. In addition, few Bosnians read papers regularly because they are expensive, and tactical teams found that posters did not appeal much to this audience. Meanwhile, newspapers, posters and leaflets constituted the core of the PSYOP effort. Likewise, in the radio field, IFOR/SFOR radios transmitted on AM while most Bosnians listened to FM radios.

---

[71] LTC John Markham, USA, SHAPE PSYOP staff officer, interview with the author, Mons, 19 December 1996.

[72] The PSYOP forces used in Bosnia an equipment adapted to third-world countries with relatively low-literacy levels, where the PSYOP community is regularly and mostly involved (Persian Gulf, Somalia, Haiti, Rwanda). This equipment, however, was not adapted to Bosnia-Herzegovina where the population is literate, relatively well-educated, and is used to most of forms of media that characterize the 'information society.'

These difficulties were compounded by the competition from local news outlets. Indeed, from the start of the operation, the CJIICTF found itself competing with the local media for visibility. According to a USIA survey released in April 1996, most Bosnians got their news from their local/ethnic media. In addition, they trusted these outlets most to get accurate news.[73] The competition only increased as normalcy returned to Bosnia-Herzegovina and local news outlets flourished. According to Media Plan, a non-profit media watchdog based in Sarajevo, more than 300 media organizations existed in Bosnia by fall 1996. Increased competition made it more difficult for the PSYOP campaign to reach its target audiences.

In response to that challenge, the CJIICTF altered its original concept. In fall 1996, the CJIICTF began to rely on the domestic media to carry IFOR's messages to the public. To avoid tampering with products by local journalists/editors, the CJIICTF provided the local media with finished products. The CJIICTF developed TV programs for local television stations to broadcast and provided local radio stations with music tapes accompanied by short messages. By the end of the IFOR mission, the CJIICTF also printed posters (ads) to be inserted in local newspapers. Resorting to local media allowed the CJIICTF to expand its coverage, and to insert its message into media which had a high level of

---

[73] U.S. Information Agency, *Public Opinion in Bosnia-Herzegovina, volume II*, Washington, D.C., Spring 1996, pp. 125-134.

credibility within the local populations. The SFOR CJICTF retained and expanded all these new means of disseminating the PSYOP message.[74]

Psychological Operations Activities

The primary mission of IFOR and SFOR Psychological Operations was to deter armed resistance and hostile behavior against IFOR/SFOR troops and operations. The PSYOP campaign was primarily conceived as a force protection tool. First, by making NATO's mandate and intentions clear to the local population and FWF, the IIC sought to prevent misunderstanding leading to unnecessary violence. Second, the IIC objective was to ensure broad compliance with the Dayton Peace Agreement and discourage the factions from interfering with IFOR/SFOR operations. The NAC themes and objectives, approved in December 1995, reflected the overwhelming importance attached to the force protection aspect of the mission. Indeed, a majority of themes emphasized that IFOR/SFOR had robust rules of engagement and the capability to enforce the peace agreement, and would respond in an even-handed manner to all violations of the peace agreement. Further themes sought to discourage the factions and local populations from hindering IFOR/SFOR operations and to encour-

---

[74] These arrangements generated a whole new set of problems. As choice for programs increased, local outlets became increasingly demanding. For example, radio stations began to place demands on the musical contents of the CJICTF's tapes or asked to be paid for airing them (selling air time as advertising time).

age cooperation with NATO. Initially, COMIFOR used these themes to encourage the factions and local populations to comply with annex 1A of the DPA.

As operations unfolded, the FWF complied, for the most part, with annex 1A of the DPA and the local population did not interfere or become openly hostile to the NATO troops. As a result, the CJIICTF began to promote themes designed to facilitate broader DPA implementation (not only annex 1A) and to get the local population to support international community activities for a successful return to peace and reconciliation. The PSYOP campaign actively supported civilian agencies operating in Bosnia-Herzegovina (mostly the OHR, the UNHCR, the UNMIBH, and the OSCE before and during the elections). Upon requests from the international organizations or upon its own initiative, the IFOR CJIICTF developed products emphasizing the importance of peace, reconstruction, and democracy. The CJIICTF developed products to explain the content of international decisions relating to peace in B-H, such as the DPA and the Brcko arbitration decision. The CJIICTF also developed a campaign in support of international organizations' work. For example, in spring 1996, the CJIICTF initiated a campaign to promote freedom of movement and encourage local populations to cross the IEBL. The IFOR CJIICTF also worked with the UN Mine Action Center (MAC) to develop mine awareness products. They were mostly designed to warn local populations (as well as IFOR troops) of the dangers caused by mines. In summer 1996, the CJIICTF actively supported the OSCE-run national elections. To that effect, the CJIICTF developed products explaining voting procedures and encouraging the local population to register and vote, and printed the material necessary for the elections to take place (such as ballots and maps of routes to polling stations).

SFOR Activities

With SFOR operations, the civilian themes component of the PSYOP campaign grew in importance. As General Crouch, USA, COMSFOR, determined that progress in the DPA civilian implementation was vital for successful mission accomplishment, the CJICTF was tasked with promoting democratic action, adherence to the rule of law, acceptance of returnees, and the ability of SFOR to enforce a secure environment in an even-handed manner. The CJICTF chose to underline themes with a slightly more aggressive approach than IFOR. The CJICTF viewed the people of Bosnia as the major proponents of change. By showing them how elected leaders should behave in a democratic country, the CJICTF hoped to raise the people's expectations toward their leaders, and ultimately, trigger major changes in the political landscape. For example, the CJICTF developed a series of products designed to explain how certain institutions (such as the military, the media, and the police) should behave in a democratic society. These products were designed to raise the population's expectations of their respective police and military forces. Likewise, the CJICTF developed a campaign in support of the elections motivating locals to vote for leaders "who will bring a brighter future." Without ever mentioning who or what parties best fit that description, the CJICTF encouraged the people to think in their long-term interests.[75] These products were designed to motivate the local populations to assert their own rights to choose and to present them with a credible alternative course of action (rather than re-electing the same leaders who would stall the peace process).

Limiting Factors

In addition to the political constraints linked to the nature of the operation (peace support operation) and discussed above, several factors limited the effectiveness of the PSYOP campaign. These factors were numerous and evolved throughout the period analyzed (December 1995 to Fall 1997). Among the most important sets of limiting factors were the nations' political sensitivities toward PSYOP and the difficulties to tailor a message adapted to the local population. This section details these factors and examines their impact on the campaign.

Reluctance Toward PSYOP

Resorting to psychological operations in support of *Operation Joint Endeavour* (December 1995) caused some unease among NATO partners. Some nations saw something of "The Manchurian Candidate" behind

---

[75] Interview with Maj. Caruso, USA, CJICTF S3, CJICTF headquarters, Sarajevo, 28 March 1997.

the PSYOP effort.[76] For example, SHAPE planners had to rename the psychological operations campaign "IFOR Information Campaign" because they feared the North Atlantic Council would not approve a plan containing the term "Psychological Operations." The SHAPE PSYOP staff officer stated that "I could not use the term 'psychological operations' when I first briefed at NATO HQ because that would have upset some nations."[77]

In addition, some of the major partners in the coalition (among them the French forces) showed reluctance at first toward the use of PSYOP forces. The French reluctance stemmed from political and historical reasons. After the defeat in Indochina (1954), the French army developed PSYOP forces and used them extensively during the Algerian conflict (1954-1962). When many of the PSYOP officers supported the *coup des généraux* in 1961 (a rebellion against the legitimate government), the Ministry of Defense disbanded all PSYOP units. This issue remains sensitive to many government officials and senior officers.[78] As a result, during *Joint Endeavour*, France only allowed a six-man U.S. PSYOP team under a bilateral liaison agreement. The U.S. team was

---

[76] "Let us face facts: PSYOP has a public-relations problem. Many organizations and individuals—from the UN to NGOs to journalists unfamiliar with the military—hear the term and an image *The Manchurian Candidate* comes to mind. This image is not simply a distortion of reality but it reflects a misunderstanding of the role of PSYOP, especially in HAOs." Adam B. Siegel, *The Role of Civil Affairs and Psychological Operations in Humanitarian Assistance Operations*, Alexandria, VA, Center for Naval Analyses, CNA Annotated Briefing 95-85.10, April 1996.

[77] Interview with LTC John Markham, USA, SHAPE PSYOP staff officer, NATO Headquarters, Brussels, 17 January 1997.

[78] However, as a result of IFOR operations, the French command for special operations (Commandement des Opérations Spéciales — COS) is now developing a PSYOP doctrine and capability.

allowed to man the IFOR radio station in Mostar. After the radio transmitter was struck down by lightning (on 14 September 1996), the U.S. liaison team was allowed to stay. It then concentrated on disseminating CJIICTF products. For most of IFOR operations, the U.S. PSYOP team was almost completely segregated from the division's staff. The U.S. forces were isolated in a remote corner of the division's HQ compound and had almost no interactions with the division's PIO, operations, or civil affairs staffs for the first six months of the operations. Although contacts improved in summer and fall 1996, the staffs were never integrated.[79]

IFOR operations did much to alleviate these fears. After a year of operations, a SHAPE PSYOP officer was allowed to talk about psychological operations without triggering a reaction. The French military decided to build a PSYOP capability. This effort coincided with the UK Ministry of Defence (MoD) authorizing the development of a British PSYOP capability (the UK development began prior to *Joint Endeavour*). However, both efforts resulted in the British and French deploying assets to conduct PSYOP during *Operation Joint Guard.*

---

[79] If the problems lies fundamentally with the French weariness about psychological operations, they were further aggravated by a clash of personalities. During the first six months of IFOR operations, the head of the PSYOP team did not want to interact with the division's staff.   Likewise, at that stage, the division's PIO also did not want to be associated with the PSYOP team. These additional problems were in part alleviated when personnel rotated in early Summer 1996. The new head of the PSYOP team, Major Chris Bailey, USA, sought better relations with the division's staff. His fluency in French helped him get along on a personal level with many of the staff officers. The new division's chief PIO, Colonel Dell'Aria, developed relationships with the PSYOP team. Interviews with Colonel Dell'Aria, USA, MND (SE) chief PIO; Maj. Chris Bailey, USA, PSYOP LNO to MND (SE); and Maj. Marconnet, FR Gen, MND (SE) PIO, Mostar, October 1996.

The Command and Control Situation

Political sensitivities not only made European nations reluctant to using PSYOP, but also complicated the command and control situation. From December 1995 to October 1997, U.S. PSYOP personnel (which formed the core of the CJIICTF) remained under national command and control. As a result of the 1984 National Security Decision Directive 130 (NSDD 130), the U.S. Department of Defense refused to place PSYOP forces under NATO command and control (C2). NSDD 130 reads:

> While U.S. international information activities must be sensitive to the concerns of foreign governments, our information programs should be understood to be a strategic instrument of U.S. national policy, not a tactical instrument of U.S. diplomacy. We cannot accept foreign control over program content.

The American refusal caused problems in everyday operations. The C2 arrangements created coordination problems as the PSYOP task force did not always feel compelled to coordinate their dissemination activities with the MND HQs. The C2 arrangement also inhibited a flexible use of PSYOP elements at the tactical level, because it only allowed the ARRC and the divisions limited authority to instruct the PSYOP personnel to conduct specific activities. In addition, as the PSYOP task forces were all-U.S. units under national C2, their logistics were to be assumed by the United States. However, as the U.S. logistical support was mainly directed toward MND (N) where the core of U.S. forces were, the PSYOP task force in Sarajevo constantly suffered from support pitfalls. It was always difficult for PSYOP elements not in MND (N) to obtain the logistical support in a timely manner. Finally, the U.S. refusal to place its PSYOP forces under NATO C2 caused tensions within the Alliance. European nations felt the PSYOP effort was not fully NATO and were therefore reluctant to become full participants. The Europeans thus pressed the U.S. to transfer authority to NATO as a prerequisite for more participation. Finally in October 1997, the U.S. DoD transferred U.S. PSYOP forces in theater to SACEUR's command and control.[80]

Approval Process

The dual chain of command had practical effects, most notably in complicating the concepts and procedures for approving PSYOP products prior to dissemination. PSYOP products were developed and approved at theater level. In theory, the PSYOP task force headquarters developed the products in accordance with the NAC's approved themes and objectives and COMIFOR/ COMSFOR approved the products before dissemination. In practice, the process was a little more complicated. Throughout the operations, various nations involved in the PSYOP effort retained review or approval authority. For example, German PSYOP forces, which developed the monthly youth magazine *Mircko*,

---

[80] This formal transfer of authority, however, did not translate into any organizational change before this monograph went to press at the end of November 1997.

had to send each issue back to Germany for a final review before dissemination. This review was established as Germany wanted to avoid any problem with its World War II legacy in the area of operations. To make sure that no material could be misinterpreted, all editions of *Mircko* went back to headquarters in Germany for final review (although not for approval). This process did not cause delays. As *Mircko* was a monthly publication, there was always time for the review process to take place without delaying publication or dissemination. In another example, all products developed by U.S. forces had to be approved both by IFOR/SFOR (NATO chain of command) and by U.S.EUCOM (U.S. chain of command). This dual procedure created conflicting requirements, as two staffs (at IFOR/SFOR and at U.S. EUCOM) had to see the final products before dissemination when the task force was under pressure to get products to target audiences as quickly as possible. In practice, this dual requirement did not seem to slow down the approval process significantly, mostly because the U.S. chain quickly agreed to a silent approval procedure whereby EUCOM would signal if products posed a problem.[81] The process was further eased as EUCOM and the CJIICTF shared a common understanding that the CJIICTF would signal in advance products that might be controversial. However good the

---

[81] When LTC Furlong, USA, deputy commander of the CJIICTF, briefed the Deputy Commander-In-Chief of U.S. Forces Europe (DCINCEUR) on 6 December 1995 regarding the IFOR product approval process, DCINCEUR agreed to delegate approval authority to COMIFOR and to rely on COMCJIICTF's day-to-day judgment in case of conflict between NATO and U.S. operations. If a conflict of interest appeared between IFOR and EUCOM's PSYOP campaigns, DCOMCJIICTF was to call EUCOM J3 to raise the issue and promote a mutually satisfying solution. Such instances, however, were rare. Comment from LTC Furlong, USA, DCOMCJIICTF from December 1995 to December 1996, Washington, D.C., 10 October 1997.

stop-gap measures were did not fix the basic problem underlying this organization: this arrangement created a de facto dual chain of command, which contradicts the basic military principle of a unified chain of command.

Additional problems occurred when LANDCENT decided to reform dramatically the theater-level approval process. Until November 1996, COMIFOR or his Chief of Staff approved the products on a routine basis. In fact, after a few months of operations, and although there was no formal transfer of control downwards, COMARRC increasingly became the approval authority. He sped up the process so that routine approval would take under 24 hours. However, upon arrival in theater, LANDCENT established a lengthy and time-consuming approval process. From then on, six staffs reviewed all PSYOP products before final approval. The JOC director, legal advisor, chief information officer, CJ2, political advisor, and PIO all reviewed and commented on the products before CJ3 or COMSFOR final approval. This lengthy process created a new set of problems. First, more time was necessary to get products approved than under the AFSOUTH/ARRC arrangement. According to Col. Schoenhaus, COMCJICTF from December 1996 to August 1997, it took 48 to 72 hours to approve a product, less than that only in case of emergency. Second, the process was burdensome as the staffs which were given an opportunity to comment felt compelled to do so. That resulted in an increased workload for what some at the CJICTF viewed as little added value. Finally, this complex approval process complicated relations between the divisions and the CJICTF headquarters, because it made it more difficult for the Task Force headquarters to respond in a timely manner to divisions' requests. This was all the more unfortunate as, throughout the operations, relations between divisions and headquarters were marked with tensions.

Relations with the MNDs

Throughout both IFOR and SFOR operations, tensions existed between the multinational divisions and the PSYOP task force headquarters. The difficulty to balance theater and divisions requirements generated these tensions. Both IFOR and SFOR insisted that the PSYOP campaign was theater-wide. This approach allowed IFOR to run a unified campaign across theater. According to LTC Furlong, DCOMCJIICTF during IFOR operations, unity of effort was essential to maintain a coherent message throughout theater. This was especially important with Bosnian Serb audiences, who were most hostile to the international community's effort and more resistant to the PSYOP message than any other Bosnian group.[82] This requirement had several implications. First, all approved products were disseminated across all three multinational divisions. Second, all PSYOP activities conducted at division level and below had to be consistent with the theater campaign.

Consistency faced challenges, however, as divisions sought more freedom to conduct their own operations. From *Joint Endeavour's* opening days, various contin-

---

[82] Comment from LTC Furlong, USA, DCOMCJIICTF from December 1995 to December 1996, Washington, D.C., 10 October 1997.

gents attempted to run their own PSYOP activities. For example, the UK-led division acquired some printing equipment in spring 1996 to develop some products specific to its AOR. In MND (SE), Spanish and Italian contingents conducted PSYOP activities in support of their CIMIC operations.[83] This tendency only increased with SFOR as non-U.S. forces decided to create or strengthen their PSYOP capabilities in Bosnia. Under SFOR, the UK-led MND (SW) published a magazine (*Mostovi*). In MND (SE), the French, German, Italian, and Spanish contingents all conducted PSYOP activities. As far as the author is aware, there was little coordination or synergy between these efforts and the CJICTF campaign.[84] Occasionally, division commanders felt that CJICTF products were not suited for their AORs and would have preferred not to have them disseminated. Although it was established in mid-1996 that subordinate commanders could not veto an approved product,[85] SFOR CJICTF personnel thought that products were not consistently disseminated across all areas.[86]

---

[83] For example, the Italian contingent developed a comic strip featuring Bugs Bunny to raise children's awareness of mines. Interview with LTC Salvatore Iacono, Italian Brigade PIO, BDE Headquarters, Zetra Stadium, Sarajevo, 23 October 1996.

[84] *Mostovi* was reviewed and approved at headquarters, but as far as other activities are concerned, it is difficult to assess if and how well headquarters was kept informed.

[85] In July 1996, Maj. Gen. Jackson, UKA, MND (SW) commander, refused to disseminate an edition of *The Herald Of Peace* featuring a front-page article on indicted war criminals with photographs of Mladic and Karadzic. Maj. Gen. Jackson felt the article was insensitive to the Bosnian Serbs. After flag-level involvement at IFOR, ARRC and EUCOM, it was decided that a division could no longer unilaterally block the dissemination of COMIFOR's approved products. Coordination mechanisms between higher and subordinate headquarters were subsequently improved to allow alterations of controversial products. Comment from LTC Furlong, USA, DCOMCJIICTF, Washington, D.C., 10 October 1997.

[86] For example, the product development chief realized that British troops in MND (SW) were not always disseminating the CJICTF products. Interview with

Division staffs also believed that the task force headquarters was not responsive to their operational needs. Early in IFOR operations, division commanders complained that products were too general for local circumstances. Throughout 1996, the ARRC encouraged the CJIICTF HQ to take greater account of local circumstances and to promote products specific to local situations. However, in the long run, these adjustments seemed unsatisfactory, especially to MND (N). First, the division's staff regularly complained that the task force headquarters did not develop products specific enough to its operational needs. According to Col. Schoenhaus, COMCJICTF from December 1996 to August 1997, some of the division's requests were not granted because the CJICTF was running a theater campaign and not a campaign on behalf of MND (N). With limited time and resources, the CJICTF focused first on COMSFOR's tasking.[87] Second, the division's staff complained that the CJICTF could not deliver products in a timely fashion. This stemmed in part from communications problems, as the CJICTF had little reliable electronic communications. For example, the CJICTF HQs could not send electronic versions of its products theaterwide. In addition, the CJICTF had difficulties communicating via e-mail with MND (N). As communications systems were streamlined through IFOR/SFOR operations to

---

Maj. Smith, CJICTF Product Development Chief from December 1996 to August 1997, CJICTF Headquarters, Sarajevo, March 1997.

[87] Interview with Col. Schoenhaus, COMCJICTF from December 1996 to August 1997, Fort Walton Beach, FL, 14 November 1997.

avoid redundancy, the communications capability was reduced, further complicating the CJICTF effort to support the divisions.

A Weak PSYOP Campaign

In addition to organizational problems, a number of factors undermined the effectiveness of the campaign. The most serious was discussed above—the very nature of a peace support operation. This meant that in Bosnia-Herzegovina, the NATO PSYOP campaign could not take actions that might undermine the parties to the DPA even though these parties themselves were often the most significant obstacles to DPA implementation. For example, in early 1997, MND (N) asked the CJICTF to develop a pamphlet discouraging reservists in the Serb army (the VRS) from reporting for duty. The CJICTF headquarters denied the request, arguing that in a peace operation they were not allowed to undermine legitimate institutions. The product was not developed. In a similar vein, the IC did not undertake efforts to directly refute the factions' regular disinformation efforts.

For the same reason, the PSYOP campaign rarely tackled difficult or controversial issues such as war criminals[88] or the fact that the parties were failing to live up

---

[88] Through July 1997, for example, the PSYOP campaign had only put one article on war criminals in *The Herald of Peace/Progress*. IFOR's reluctance to deal with indicted war criminals went as far as modifying a poster printed on behalf of the ICTY. The original poster identified all publicly indicted war criminals with their last known addresses. After journalists challenged the U.S. military's claim that it had insufficient intelligence to arrest the war criminals by pointing to the addresses on the poster (reporters had been able to locate 12 of the indicted war criminals just using this information), IFOR reprinted the poster without the addresses. The decision outraged the ICTY which asked that its logo be removed from the poster.

to the agreement they had signed. The NATO leadership feared that addressing such controversial issues
might lead to resentment against or hostility to the force.
Thus, for example, the PSYOP campaign promoted the
freedom of movement across the IEBL, but did not address the fact that the parties (the officials of the entities) were often a major part of the reason that such
travel was not safe for non-international civilians. These
restrictions were well recognized by many within the
PSYOP community in Bosnia but they stated that their
orders prevented them from executing a more aggressive campaign.[89]   The conciliatory tone of the PSYOP
campaign dismayed many in the international community working in Bosnia. For example, OHR officials commented that they had little use for a campaign that was
too weak to have substantial impact. Duncan Bullivan,
public affairs officer at the OHR, explained: "We are at a
point where we point fingers at people who block the
process, but SFOR is not involved in that."[90] This was
perhaps the chief factor contributing to a feeling in the
international organizations that the PSYOP campaign
was ineffective. Even if it was the chief factor, however,

At the end of this controversy, IFOR decided not to distribute the posters which had
omitted the addresses. See, Colin Soloway, "How not to catch a war criminal," *U.S.
News and World Report*, 9 December 1996, p 63.

[89] It is unclear to what extent this was a self-fulfilling prophesy. PSYOP
personnel produced more aggressive products "as practice" and for their own
"amusement" but didn't bother to pass them up the chain of command assuming that
they would be rejected out-of-hand by COMIFOR/COMSFOR (if not before that level).
Based on interviews with CJIICTF/CJICTF personnel in Fall 1996 and Spring 1997.

[90] Interview with Duncan Bullivan, OHR public affairs officer, OHR
headquarters, Sarajevo, 1 April 1997. His views were echoed at the UNMIBH and the
UNHCR.

it was not the only one. The following paragraphs discuss other factors limiting PSYOP effectiveness that were under the control of the PSYOP task force.

Difficult Adaptation to the Cultural Environment

As in any other operation, the PSYOP community needed to adapt its message to its target audience. For its message to be effective, the PSYOP campaign needed to use arguments relevant to the local cultures and to present them in a way that would appeal to target audiences. This was difficult to achieve as the PSYOP campaign lacked regional experts and adequate resources to determine the populations' expectations. Beginning in 1996, a civilian regional expert (a contracted Ph.D. candidate at Columbia University) was assigned to the IFOR CJIICTF. He remained with the SFOR CJICTF. However, this expert was seconded to various international organizations to work on projects such as the OHR independent TV network (1996) and the OSCE voter education program (1997) rather than being integrated into the PSYOP Task Force production staff. In addition, little reliable data (such as polling data or focus groups) existed on local population attitudes and expectations to help the PSYOP effort. During 1996, USIA conducted four polls in Bosnia-Herzegovina. However, as far as the author has been able to determine, the results were not communicated in a timely fashion to the IFOR CJIICTF. The situation improved slightly during the SFOR period, as the CJICTF was able to track down several studies (such as the result of focus groups conducted in late 1996) and polling data. From these data, the CJICTF decided that economic issues (such as reconstruction) and multi-ethnicity were two issues the Bosnians valued. It was especially important to determine such issues, as "persuasive communication usually has its greatest effect in reinforcement rather than conversion."[91] To alleviate these problems, the PSYOP task force tried to pre-test products before dissemination. The process consisted of asking locals working for the CJICTF for their reactions. It also consisted of asking TPTs to conduct some testing in their AORs. However, the scale and sophistication of the pre-testing was insufficient to compensate for the lack of regional expertise.

Lack of strong regional expertise and available cultural data generated some problems, such as products not adapted to the local environment. For example, during 1996, the CJIICTF developed a "checklist" of what was done and what had to be achieved. After the product was disseminated, the CJIICTF realized that Bosnians don't do checklists. In another example, they developed a poster with a chess game to encourage voting. Bosnians interpreted it as the international community playing with Bosnia's future. Other products did not take into account the local population's knowledge and were, perhaps, too Americanized. For example, SFOR developed several products on the role of the military, the police, and the media in a democracy. These products

[91] Daniel Lerner, "Is International Persuasion Sociologically Feasible" in Department of the Army, *The Art and Science of Psychological Operations: Case Studies of Military Application*, volume 1, pamphlet no. 525-7-1, Washington, D.C., April 1976, p. 47.

used quotes from Western historic figures (for example, Lincoln, Roosevelt, Clausewitz, or Clemenceau), which some did not believe appropriate for Bosnia-Herzegovina. These products did not appeal to the Bosnians' culture or history, nor did they dwell on recent examples of national reconciliation or mediation (such as Salvador or South Africa). This limited the PSYOP products' relevance to their target audiences.

Working With International Organizations

Undertaking a successful campaign in support of the international organizations was another challenge. Supporting the international organizations was an unusual task. PSYOP forces rarely operate closely with international and non-governmental organizations. During *Joint Endeavour* and *Joint Guard*, however, supporting civilian organizations constituted a large part of the PSYOP work. But the CJICTF encountered many difficulties in establishing and maintaining fruitful relationships with international organizations.

A first challenge was to establish an effective PSYOP/civilian agencies interface for communicating requirements and capabilities between these organizations. Throughout the operations, the PSYOP task forces had limited access to the international organizations and little information about their operations. In addition, the task forces did not successfully "market" themselves as a valuable ally to the IO/NGOs' staffs. For the most part, the task forces advertised their technical capability and free qualified labor force, but failed to market their expertise, e.g., the ability to conduct a step-by-step campaign designed to achieve attitudinal change.   As a consequence of this weak liaison and coordination structure, and limited understanding on both sides, a number of problems existed throughout the operations.

- There were several breakdowns in support. Civilian organizations were not always able to formulate clear requirements.[92] Sometimes they formulated their requirements incorrectly, thus undermining their own objectives.[93]
- The PSYOP task force did not understand the requirements and constraints the international organizations were operating under. In particular, PSYOP personnel often failed to realize that civilian organizations often depended on the factions' willingness to establish policy before they could announce anything. Before they could prepare a product (for elections, returns, or demining), the civilian organizations first had to obtain from the factions a policy statement. Sometimes, civilian organizations could not provide the information the CJICTF needed in a timely fashion. This hindered effective PSYOP support.[94]

---

[92] For example, in October 1996, the UNHCR announced at a JICC meeting it was launching a campaign in favor of refugee returns to the Zone of Separation. The CJIICTF immediately offered to help design the campaign and disseminate the products. For that, the CJIICTF asked the UNHCR to provide its campaign plan. For several months, the UNHCR was unable to produce a plan summarizing the agreed-upon policy. Author's notes from JICC meetings, IFOR Press Center, Sarajevo, 14 and 21 October 1996.

[93] For example, the UN Mine Action Center asked the CJIICTF to develop a product asking people to report unexploded mines to their headquarters. To that effect, they asked that their phone number be placed on the poster. However, the MAC only mentioned a number in Sarajevo, only available when calling from the Bosniac part of the territory. The poster's utility was thus considerably reduced.

[94] This was certainly the case with OSCE. During both the national and municipal election campaigns, PSYOP personnel felt especially frustrated with what they believed was the OSCE's inability to present the information it needed to put

- International organizations used the PSYOP campaign as a one-shot tool to develop one or two products but not for long-term campaigns, those most likely to achieve attitudinal change.

A second challenge stemmed from different civilian and military planning and action cycles. The military is generally more planning oriented than civilian organizations, while the latter deal more in the immediacy. Although many in the military seem to believe this derived from civilian incompetence, it relates far more to differing resource availability and missions. For the military, a key responsibility is to plan for contingency. Thus the military allocates substantial resources to a formal planning process. Civilian organizations, however, develop their concept or goal and deal with events as they unfold. In addition, few civilian organizations have enough resources to dedicate significant numbers of people to planning and few organizations have planning cycles as well-defined and formalized as the U.S. and NATO military structures have developed.[95] These differences in cycle meant that civilian and military organizations

---

forward to inform voters in a timely fashion. They pointed out to many examples. During the national election campaign (August-September 1996), the OSCE asked the CJIICTF to develop a map of the 19 cross-IEBL routes for voters to use on election day. However, it took 2 weeks and 12 changes before the OSCE approved the product. In consequence, "the map was not as widely distributed as it could have been and not many people saw it." (Interview with Maj. Gallo, CJIICTF product development cell, CJIICTF Headquarters, Sarajevo, 15 October 1996.) In fact, the routes were constantly reworked by the factions. Similar delays occurred during the campaign for voter registration for the municipal elections (March-April 1997). Says Debra Weltz, a strategic analyst for the SFOR CJICTF seconded to OSCE, "When I ask for information, it is never available or complete. There is always something missing." (Interview with the author, OSCE headquarters, 27 March 1997.) In fact, the OSCE depended on the factions to set the policy, which took numerous endless meetings.

[95] For example, the entire UNHCR staff throughout Bosnia-Herzegovina in Spring 1997 numbered about 130, or less than 20% of HQ SFOR and 0.5% of all SFOR. The UNHCR was one of the largest civilian organizations operating in Bosnia.

had different expectations of what can and should be done and how it should be done. These different cycles also led to mutual bitter complaints and gave the misguided impression that support was not working.

A final challenge consisted of developing a message that fit both the IOs and IFOR/SFOR needs. Each organization had its own agenda and priorities and these were not always in full accord. Product development and approval process allowed IFOR/SFOR to ensure that the PSYOP campaign would not support international organization requests in contradiction with the commander's goals and objectives. [96] However, the process did not ensure that civilian organizations approved, or even were kept informed of campaigns that affected their areas of responsibilities. Many IFOR/SFOR products had the potential to affect the civilian organizations' work. Indeed, both task forces developed numerous products supporting various aspects of civilian implementation as part of the commander's campaign. For example, COMSFOR tasked the SFOR CJICTF to develop campaigns supporting a secure environment (SFOR responsibility), displaced persons and refugees (UNHCR responsibility), common institutions (OHR responsibility), economic recovery (civilian organizations responsibility), and elections (OSCE responsibility). In addition, even products developed in support of SFOR responsibilities could affect the civilian organizations' posture. As these campaigns supported COMSFOR's

---

[96] For example, the ICRC asked the CJICTF to help disseminate a poster. The poster featured a pair of eyes wide open and asked people to report missing persons. The CJICTF, however, thought the poster was too provocative and denied the ICRC's request for support.

plan, they were neither developed in concert with nor approved by the international organizations. The messages, tone, and timeliness were left at IFOR/SFOR's discretion.

The process for developing and approving products that potentially affected the IOs' responsibilities thus left room for error and misunderstanding. Indeed, such products could easily contradict the civilian organizations' messages. It seems, however, that the civilian organizations did not pay much attention to this problem. Interviews conducted in March/April 1997 revealed that civilian organizations were not aware of most CJICTF products. Their attitude seemed to have less to do with the process, rather than with their views of the CJICTF campaign's effectiveness. OHR, UNHCR, and UNMIBH personnel commented to the author that they had little use for a campaign that was too weak to have any substantial impact. They viewed it as something to cooperate with, but not worth expending significant efforts. The civilian organizations thus were not troubled that they did not have a say in the campaign because most of the material appeared to them as non-controversial. Indeed, the author is only aware of one instance where the High Representative asked COMSFOR not to disseminate a product.

The Difficulty of Assessing PSYOP Effectiveness

Adaptation to the local environment was all the more difficult because PSYOP had difficulties assessing the campaign's impact. First, it is difficult to measure the real impact of any communication. Research shows that communication's impact is almost never direct. Establishing a direct link between a message and a specific attitude is therefore difficult. On top of these scientific limitations, the IFOR and SFOR PSYOP did not have adequate resources (in terms or manpower and qualifications) to conduct an effective assessment of their impact.

The PSYOP task forces conducted pre- and post-testing to assess the campaigns' impact on the local populations. Pre-testing measures included all steps taken to test the products before dissemination. As part of the pre-testing program, most products were checked by locals working within headquarters (most notably for adequacy and language) before production. When resources were available, tactical teams in the field randomly tested some products (such as posters) among the local population and provided feedback to headquarters. In some cases, pre-testing led to some products being modified before dissemination. These measures, however, remained mostly informal and limited, due to a lack of resources and time. In addition, both task forces conducted post-testing measures to assess the impact of each product after dissemination. Such measures consisted of standard impact indicators developed for each product and documented by the tactical teams during the dissemination missions. Table 3 provides a summary of the types of indicators, along with definitions and examples.

Table 3: Psychological Operations Impact Indicators (post-testing measures)

Measure of Effectiveness	Definition	Example
Production	Addresses individual actions taken by the force.	110,000 copies of The Herald of Peace distributed weekly; 25 TV spots produced.
Acceptance rate	Captures the people's reaction when presented with PSYOP products	TPT on a dissemination mission register people's reactions when handed the material (pleasure or displeasure; acceptance or refusal; friendly or aggressive behavior). CJICTF pays attention to community leaders' reactions. TPT conducts small-scale polls.
Behavioral change	Registers whether the local populations changed their behavior after a particular campaign	A campaign is launched to raise people's awareness on mines. The campaign leads to a behavioral change if the number of mine casualties decreases after the campaign is disseminated.

Such measures, however, only imperfectly measured the PSYOP campaign's effectiveness because they did not document the full impact of the mission.

- Level-of-effort measures provided insights into the magnitude of the PSYOP effort. Such measures were easy to document accurately. IFOR and SFOR therefore regularly provided updates on their efforts, listing how many products were developed and disseminated.[97]
- Acceptance rate was important to document. Product acceptance is a prerequisite to potential impact. If people refuse exposure to the material distributed, they cannot be influenced. To document the acceptance of its products, IFOR and SFOR PSYOP tactical forces used several indicators. They gathered anecdotal evidence from discussions with locals encountered during the dissemination missions; documented community leaders' reactions; and conducted small-scale polls. According to PSYOP personnel, the generally positive attitude of the locals during dissemination missions and a number of openly hostile officials' reactions to PSYOP material indicated that their campaign had a positive effect. In fact, the measures used do not fully support that conclusion because acceptance rate does not document the impact.

---

[97] As of March 1997, IFOR and SFOR CJICTF had disseminated 1,194,100 handbills; 1,646,410 posters; 6,085,000 newspapers (for 57 editions); 395,000 Mircko (for 8 editions); 1375 radio programs, 51 television broadcasts, and numerous miscellaneous articles such as coloring books, soccer balls, pens and writing pads. Combined Joint Information Campaign Task Force, *Command Brief: Operation Joint Guard*, NATO UNCLASSIFIED, Sarajevo, 4 March 1997.

• Documenting behavioral changes was maybe the most significant measure, but also the most difficult. Indeed, data was not always available to compare behaviors before and after a specific campaign. In addition, these measures were only possible for a handful of campaigns, such as mine awareness, freedom of movement, or illegal police checkpoints. In each of these categories, NATO could establish statistics reflecting the locals' behavior before and after the campaign. Such measures were more difficult to undertake with most campaigns supporting democracy, reconstruction, or reconciliation.

Although none of these measures were illegitimate, they only portrayed a partial assessment of the campaign's impact. These measures did not indicate how people perceived issues and how the PSYOP campaign affected those perceptions. Interviews with IFOR CJIICTF personnel revealed that PSYOP personnel were aware of the measures' limitations. *The Herald of Peace* editor stated: "My feel is that we have a good impact, but it is very difficult to measure the effectiveness of some of our campaigns."[98] A PSYOP officer at MND (SW) concurred: "MOE is a very difficult issue. We try to conduct polls, but we rely on small samples. There are a lot of people we are not seeing. We don't have the resources to conduct large scale assessment."[99] In addition to the measures conducted, PSYOP needed to conduct mis-

---

[98] Interview with Maj. Mason, USA, *The Herald Of Peace* editor, CJIICTF headquarters, Sarajevo, 12 October 1996.

[99] Interview with PSYOP officer, MND (SW) headquarters, Banja-Luka, 14 October 1996.

sion-level measures designed to "address progress made toward the political objectives set forth for the mission."[100] As a result, it is very difficult to provide an accurate assessment of the PSYOP campaign.

Conclusion

PSYOP was entrusted with a vital mission in a difficult environment: provide an honest alternate viewpoint in a sea of local propaganda and disinformation to facilitate DPA implementation. However, three sets of factors limited the effectiveness of the PSYOP campaign. First, political sensitivities surrounding the use of PSYOP forces made it more difficult to run an effective, multinational PSYOP campaign. Second, the weak and conciliatory nature of the PSYOP message limited its potential impact on the local populations. The task forces' difficulties in adapting to the local culture and media habits further impaired the campaign. Finally, these shortcomings were all the more difficult to correct as PSYOP's assessment of its effort was at best limited.

---

[100] John Nelson et al., *Measures of Effectiveness for Humanitarian Assistance Operations*, Center for Naval Analyses, CRM 95-166.10, April 1996.

Chapter 4:
CIMIC Information
Activities

In addition to PI and PSYOP, IFOR and SFOR Civil-
Military Cooperation (CIMIC) units were also tasked
with conducting information activities. CIMIC, composed almost exclusively of U.S. Army reserve civil affairs, acted as the interface between NATO and civilian
organizations (both local and international) working in
Bosnia-Herzegovina. According to the OPLAN, CIMIC
units were tasked to publicize their activities in the local
and international press. This covers traditional public
information activities designed to promote CIMIC operations. Second, the units were tasked to provide information to aid the local populations (civil information).
Civil information involved, for example, warning populations about an outbreak of rabies or educating them
about the dangers caused by mines. Although U.S. civil
affairs units are familiar with these activities, they are
not yet part of the developing NATO CIMIC doctrine.
However, as the CIMIC units were mainly composed of
U.S. personnel, they conducted these activities according to U.S. doctrine and practices. This chapter briefly

discusses the IFOR Combined Joint Civil-Military Co-operation (CJCIMIC) and SFOR Civil-Military Task Force (CMTF) information activities.

IFOR CJCIMIC Information Activities

During IFOR operations, civil-military cooperation was principally the responsibility of a 300-personnel unit called the Combined Joint Civil-Military Cooperation (CJCIMIC). The CJCIMIC was both the staff component and advisor to COMIFOR on civil-military issues and a unit whose personnel conducted civil-military activities throughout theater. The CJCIMIC commander designated a lieutenant-colonel (USA) to deal with public and civil information activities. He was tasked to publicize the unit's activities (in particular with the local press); disseminate all information that might help the local populations; and help in the democratization of the Bosnian media.[101]   In addition, the LTC sought to coordinate CJCIMIC information activities with PI and PSYOP. To achieve these goals, CJCIMIC adopted a proactive policy and tried to stimulate media interest in its activities and operations. Among its regular activities, the CJCIMIC chief of civil information—

- Maintained an updated list of the unit's activities for general information. The list was forwarded to the Sarajevo CPIC every week for further dissemination.

[101] Interview with LTC Brune, USA, Chief of Civil Information, CJCIMIC headquarters, Sarajevo, 15 October 1996.

- Set up regular media opportunities to publicize the unit's achievements. Such opportunities included inviting all interested journalists to the Sarajevo/Gorazde track inauguration or to the Sarajevo tramway inauguration. These opportunities were designed to demonstrate progress in the reconstruction of Bosnia-Herzegovina.
- Issued regular press communiqués to publicize CIMIC activities and disseminate information to aid the local population.
- Wrote articles in *The Herald Of Peace*.

In addition, the CJICIMIC chief of civil information was involved in different programs designed to promote media democratization across Bosnia-Herzegovina. In that regard, CJCIMIC worked closely with the OHR on the Open Broadcast Network (OBN).[102] He also worked closely with the OSCE media development program to run an inter-entity editors group where journalists and editors from all parties (Bosniacs, Bosnian Serbs, and Bosnian Croats) held seminars to discuss free and fair reporting and standards of ethics and professionalism. Four such meetings took place in the course of 1996.

The CJCIMIC information activities encountered numerous obstacles along the road. LTC Brune assessed that civil information campaigns (such as warning about a disease outbreak or informing of disturbance caused by IFOR operations) helped the local communities. On at least several occasions, locals undertook sanitary

---

[102] The OBN is a network of Bosnian television stations producing and exchanging programs. The network, sponsored by the international community, strives to promote an independent voice among the faction-controlled media.

precautions following CJCIMIC actions. However, the public information campaign quickly faced a major obstacle: "good news doesn't sell." As a result, CIMIC operations did not attract major attention from the international press corps (especially in Sarajevo, where there were major policy issues debated). In mid-October 1996, BGEN Deloatch (USA), CJCIMIC Commander, expressed his dissatisfaction with the lack of coverage his unit was receiving. Squadron Leader Nigel Branston, UKA, from IFOR PI, summarized the situation: "The CIMIC is good news and the media is not interested in good news. In addition, small projects such as rebuilding a bridge or a school don't interest them. We advertise their activities, but the media won't pick it up."[103] Lastly, in terms of its contribution to media democratization, LTC Brune had no illusions:

> It is very difficult to judge these programs' effectiveness. Although we reach out to local journalists and editors and try to improve their professional standards, you can't know whether you are impacting on them. It is very difficult to determine whether we alter or not their behavior. Journalists here are still under the factions' control.[104]

---

[103] Author's notes from IFOR HQ, Public Information morning staff meeting, Sarajevo, 21 October 1996.

[104] Interview with LTC Brune, CJCIMIC chief civil information, CJCIMIC headquarters, Sarajevo, 15 October 1996.

The SFOR CIMIC Information Activities

The Civil-Military Cooperation was reorganized in November 1996 with the transition between AFSOUTH/ ARRC and LANDCENT. Based on a recommendation from BGEN Deloatch, the unit and staff component activities were dissociated. In November 1996, LANDCENT established a CJ9 to serve as advisor to the commander and planner on civil military issues. CJ9 had three elements: its multinational staff component; a CIMIC center based in Sarajevo designed to be the principal linkage between SFOR and the civilian organizations who did not have a permanent representation from or to SFOR; and a Civil-Military Task Force (CMTF) in charge of assisting reconstruction and rehabilitation, principally around Sarajevo. Further changes occurred as a new U.S. Army reserve civil affairs unit rotated into theater in early December 1996. At that stage, changes were mostly personality related. According to interviews with civil affairs personnel, the relation between the CJ9 elements and the CMTF commander went from cooperative to antagonistic and competitive, creating a deleterious working environment.

CIMIC information activities suffered through this evolution. Planners tasked the CJ9 staff with conducting CIMIC information activities. However, the CJ9 had neither the resources nor the expertise to carry out this tasking effectively. The CMTF (which had the resources, and at least in part, the expertise) conducted minimal activities in that realm. The CMTF commander, Col. Michael Beasley, USAR, did not seem to place much emphasis on the subject. Indeed, the personnel in charge of information activities were not as senior as in the previous rotation. Rather than a lieutenant-colonel, a captain was assigned the information activities responsibilities and then reassigned to other duties), thus signaling a reduced interest. Later, Col. Beasley assigned one NCO (a sergeant) to act as the Public Information Officer for the unit and assigned another one to civil information.

This structure was insufficient to conduct effective CIMIC information activities. Working with one junior NCO with no experience in public information, the CMTF public affairs officer (PAO) did not have the time or resources to do anything other than command information (in the form of a monthly bulletin on and for the task force and their families). He thus had no time to contribute to civil information or even to conduct basic media relations. "There is much to do in these arenas, but I don't have time to dig up stories and sell them to the press." In addition, he outlined: "I can't send press releases regularly because I don't get the stories in a timely fashion. If I get a story five days after it occurred, then it is not worth anything for the media." [105]   As for civil information, the picture is even easier to draw: there was none. Although an NCO was assigned to do civil information on behalf of the task force, the author is unaware of any activity in that field. With this in mind, it should not be

---

[105] Interview with Staff Sergeant Helton, USAR, CMTF PAO, CMTF headquarters, Sarajevo, 3 April 1997.

surprising that there was no meaningful coordination between the CMTF and the PI/PSYOP campaign through the first six months of SFOR operations.[106]

The lack of communication on the part of the CMTF became clear when in June 1997, Secretary of State Madeleine Albright said she wanted SFOR to do more in the civilian implementation. In reaction, SFOR set up a special press conference featuring the CMTF commander. Asked to react to the Secretary's comments, Col. Beasley answered:

> We sent her a note shortly after her speech, General Crouch did, that elaborated more on exactly how busy we are. Frankly, it also helps us within our international organizations to be rather invisible. We don't try to beat our chests, we don't try to greatly broadcast our role within the civil implementation. We very much prefer to go in quietly, stealthily as it were, and do our job and extract ourselves in an appropriate manner. Part of the reason for this press conference today, though was to make sure that more people understood this largely invisible role that we are playing towards civil implementation.[107]

---

[106] The CJICTF attempted several times to kick-start cooperation, including giving a CJICTF command briefing to CMTF staff. However, these attempts did not lead to any fruitful cooperation. This disconnect existed even though the two elements shared the same buildings and had offices interspersed with each other.

[107] Col. W. Michael Beasley, Civil-Military Task Force, 24 June 1997. Press Conference at the Coalition Press Information Center, Holiday Inn, Sarajevo. Sent by NATO public data service, "NATO/SFOR: LANDCENT transcript of third Press Briefing, June 24, 1997" on 25 June 1997.

Conclusion

Throughout the NATO operations, effectively publiciz-
ing CIMIC activities proved a challenge as CIMIC activities did not arouse media interest. In spite of its efforts
to publicize its activities, IFOR CJCIMIC found that neither the international nor local media accurately reflected
its contributions to rebuilding Bosnia. The situation only
got worse with the new rotation of CA unit in December
1996 as the new CIMIC leadership concentrated on
command information and did not actively seek to publicize the unit's operations. At that point, SFOR CIMIC
activities were essentially invisible to the international
and local publics. Hoping that the people would understand the CIMIC's invisible role, as Colonel Beasley put
it in his June 1997 declaration, was thus impossible.

Chapter 5:
Coordinating
Information Activities

Effective communication in Bosnia-Herzegovina required that all purveyors of information disseminate a coherent message in line with what actually occurred on the ground. To ensure message coherence, the commander's information activities within the command had to be closely associated and coordinated with international organizations. However, ensuring coordination was a major challenge. The DPA implementation involved a 36-nation military coalition (IFOR), at least five major organizations (NATO, OHR, UNHCR, OSCE, UNMIBH), and several hundreds of other organizations. Like IFOR/SFOR, most of these organizations had proactive information policies. In addition, three staff components within IFOR/SFOR headquarters (PI, PSYOP, and CIMIC information) worked on information activities. Ensuring harmony and cohesion of message was thus a difficult task. It was achieved through a variety of meetings where information policy and activities were discussed, and NATO's information strategy for theater was established. This chapter first examines the principles enabling a close association of all information activities within the command, then describes the mechanisms set up to ensure message coherence, and concludes with an examination of the benefits and difficulties of establishing fruitful cooperation. Because the mechanisms evolved from IFOR to SFOR operations, this section examines separately the mechanisms set up during *Joint Endeavour* and *Joint Guard*.

The Association of PI/PSYOP/CIMIC Information

Many officers throughout NATO operations in B-H praised the close association between Public Information, Psychological Operations, and CIMIC information. In fact, the unusual aspect most praised was the association between PI and PSYOP.[108] Traditionally, PI and PSYOP activities are separated. The strict separation stems from different missions and philosophies.

- Psychological Operations are an operational tool (under G/J3-operations-supervision) designed to influence target audiences' perceptions and shape their behaviors in favor of one's troops and operations.
- Public information, on the other hand, has a dual function. First, public information is an operational tool designed to gain and maintain public opinion support for the operation. It is also used as a public diplomacy tool designed to communicate with and pres-

---

[108] CIMIC information, as explained earlier, did not play a critical role in IFOR/SFOR information activities. See chapter 4, CIMIC information activities.

sure adversaries into a friendly course of action. Second, public information results from a basic democratic requirement. It is the means by which a commander reports to the people what their children and tax dollars are used for. It is one means by which a commander is held accountable for his actions by the ultimate source of democratic legitimacy: the public. This democratic requirement entails some obligations, such as truthful and timely reporting within constraint of operational security.

Because of the democratic requirement underlying the public affairs mission, PIOs are generally reluctant to be associated with operations designed to influence attitudes (sometimes through disinformation or deception). For PIOs, being associated with such operations would inevitably damage their credibility with journalists. However, the reality of today's communications renders the strict separation between PSYOP and PI difficult to maintain. For example, a PSYOP message disseminated to a local audience may be picked up by reporters and broadcast through the national and international media. Conversely, a message intended for the international media may be heard by the local population if they have access to foreign media or if the local press also reports the PI material. It is thus difficult to maintain a strict separation between the two activities.

The nature of *Operation Joint Endeavour*, a peace operation, made it possible to closely associate public information and psychological operations. The IFOR PSYOP campaign consisted of convincing the local population (and incidentally the FWF) of the benefits of the Dayton agreement by relying on true arguments. IFOR/SFOR ran a straightforward PSYOP campaign emphasizing the benefits of democratization and reconstruction and stressing multi-ethnicity. To carry out its campaign, IFOR and SFOR did not resort to deception or disinformation campaigns (which might occur in a warfighting environment). Under these circumstances, PSYOP and PI relied on similar arguments and themes. Each staff was entrusted with reaching a specific audience (see figure 8: PI/PSYOP division of labor). PI dealt with local, national, and international journalists. PSYOP carried the IFOR/SFOR message to the local population without the mediation of journalists.

IFOR Coordination Mechanisms

Internal Coordination

Internal coordination was designed to enhance information flow between staff components, avoid diverging strategies and duplication of efforts, and synchronize activities so they mutually reinforced each other. This internal coordination made it less likely that different staff components would develop divergent plans and activities. Plans established several coordination forums, which IFOR and ARRC further developed once in theater. The most important mechanisms were as follows.

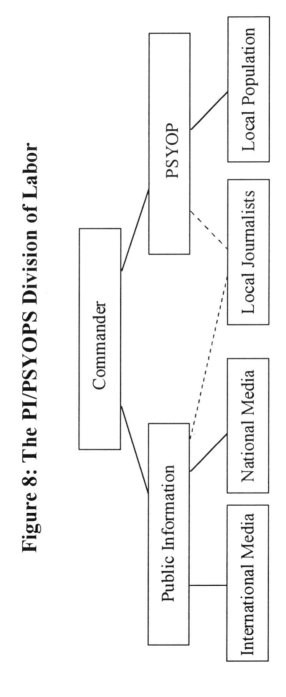

Figure 8: The PI/PSYOPS Division of Labor

The Chief Information Officer: Shortly after deployment, the ARRC Commander (COMARRC) designated a Chief Information Officer (CIO) and tasked him with organizing the daily coordination between the PI and the CJIICTF staffs at operational level. On a daily basis, the CIO developed a centralized coordination process to ensure that all messages flowing out of IFOR conformed to the commander's intent, were coherent with one another, and reinforced each other in a timely manner. The CIO had direct access to COMARRC and exercised authority over the ARRC PI. However, he had no authority over the CJIICTF, as the PSYOP unit (for all practical purposes) was under U.S. command and control.[109] In spite of these difficulties, the CIO remained a central point within headquarters for sharing and exchanging information and developing and timing information campaigns.

The ARRC Information Coordination Group: Daily coordination principally took place at the Information Coordination Group (ICG). Every morning, COMARRC chaired an ICG composed of the ARRC Chief of Staff, civilian political advisor, his civilian media advisor, CIO, IFOR chief PIO, ARRC spokesmen, the deputy commander of the CJIICTF (DCOMCJIICTF), ARRC G3, and G5/civil affairs. In practice, however, IFOR PIO did not always attend the ARRC meeting. The ICG decided which message to put forward that day, and chose the delivery system (media and/or PSYOP) and the timing of the delivery.

---

[109] See chapter 3: Psychological Operations.

The ARRC Perception Group: Every Friday, the ARRC CIO chaired a perception group meeting. IFOR CPIO and DCPIO, ARRC spokesmen, DCOMCJIICTF, ARRC G3, and G5/civil affairs attended the meeting. They looked at media coverage trends and determined how best to present and time IFOR's arguments to the media. The group worked on a two-to-four week horizon and produced a weekly information matrix summarizing all information activities throughout theater.

The ARRC Crisis Planning Group: This group met as crises erupted for contingency planning. This meeting brought PI and PSYOP planners into operational planning at an early moment.

Although the coordination mechanisms established at HQ levels proved to be beneficial, most notably by enhancing the information flow, they were not necessarily reproduced at division levels. At that level, the coordination mechanisms varied considerably. Coordination mechanisms were established at MND (N) and MND (SW). The U.S.-led MND (N) held an Information Operations Council designed to bring together the key players relevant for information dissemination (PAO, J3, PSYOP, and civil affairs). In the UK-led MND (SW), although the chief PIO did not organize a specific coordination forum, he kept in close contact with the PSYOP unit (located across the hall from his office) and attended operational and civil affairs meetings. Coordination was thus mostly informal, through walk-ins and phone calls with relevant staff. It is unclear whether the MND (SW) informal approach would have been more effective associated with formal coordination mechanisms.[110] The French-led MND (SE), on the other hand, did not mirror the internal coordination mechanisms and forums set up at headquarters. The division commanders seemed to consider information a support activity. As a result, there were no formal coordination processes linking the PIO to the rest of the staff. At first, the PIO was not even invited to sit and listen to the morning and evening conference calls. Throughout the operation, PI neither chaired nor participated in coordination meetings with other staff elements. As the operation progressed, the PI officers established informal links with the American PSYOP liaison team, the G5 (civil affairs), and the G3. However, the division's PIOs found it difficult to work under these circumstances, and stated that much depended on the personalities involved. As a result, internal coordination remained loose throughout the year.

External Coordination

Coordination also took place with primary civilian organizations in charge of facilitating the DPA civilian implementation, in particular the OHR, the UNHCR, the OSCE, and the UNMIBH. Occasional coordination also took place with other organizations such as the World Bank and the International Criminal Tribunal for former Yugoslavia (ICTY).[111] The operations benefited greatly

---

[110] While the MND (SW) operated in an intimate and rather collegial atmosphere, it is notable that the PI and PSYOP offices were in a separate building from most of the command group.

[111] We call primary civilian organizations the international organizations tasked to facilitate the implementation of major aspects of the Dayton Peace Agreement:

from the external coordination, although it took some time for all the organizations involved to develop effective cooperation mechanisms.

Establishing fruitful coordination mechanisms was difficult. Early in *Joint Endeavour*, IFOR felt that coordinating with the civilian agencies was necessary for its own sake. By the end of February 1996, as implementation of annex 1A went more smoothly than expected, IFOR PI realized that media interest was shifting to the civilian implementation of the DPA. However, at that stage, the primary civilian organizations attended, but did not take part in the daily briefing. The IFOR CPIO believed this inappropriately led IFOR to talk about civilian issues that were outside IFOR's realm of responsibility. The IFOR CPIO feared that this situation could damage IFOR credibility. IFOR PI thus began to establish coordination mechanisms with the civilian agencies. This proved a challenging task.

First, civilian agencies were slow to respond to IFOR's offers for cooperation as many arrived in theater well after IFOR had deployed. For a while, civilian agencies were consumed by problems in setting up their own operations.[112] Therefore, cooperation with IFOR PI was not their main concern. In addition, the relations between IFOR and the OHR (principal civilian facilitator) had a rocky start which did not contribute to a trusting

---

the OHR (as main coordinator), the UNHCR (on refugees issues), the UNMIBH (on police and justice), and the OSCE (on elections).

[112] Most of the international organizations faced numerous logistical problems setting up their operations, in particular funding, personnel, and equipment problems.

climate between NATO and the civilian community. It also seemed that some of the civilian organizations were reluctant to cooperate closely with IFOR out of fear they would lose their freedom of speech and be tainted by their association with a military force. As a result, widespread cooperation was not fully in place before mid-May 1996.[113]

The daily combined briefing: In early spring 1996, the OHR, the UNHCR, the UNMIBH, and the OSCE agreed to brief the press along with IFOR daily at the Holiday Inn. On occasion, other civilian organizations such as the World Bank or the ICRC joined the briefing. The IFOR Sarajevo press center thus became the focal point for dissemination of information about the international effort in Bosnia-Herzegovina. Anyone seeking information about the peace process could find the principal international interlocutors at the Sarajevo Holiday Inn and had at their disposal there a substantial amount of information on the international community's work in Bosnia-Herzegovina. With the daily combined briefings, the international community sought to present itself as united in a common effort in support of the DPA implementation. The major organizations did not seek (or pretend) to present a single approach and regularly presented differing views of events. Major points of controversy included NATO's role in maintaining civil

---

[113] According to Col. Charles de Noirmont, FRA, IFOR DCPIO between December 1995 and July 1996, Admiral Smith threatened the major international organizations with withdrawing IFOR support for the Sarajevo Holiday Inn Press Center (where the daily briefings were organized) if the civilian agencies did not assume more responsibilities. Following this, the agencies accepted to take partial charge of the briefing and chair the daily briefing three times a week. Interview with the author, Paris, 19 November 1996.

order or in arresting indicted war criminals. However, by agreeing to brief together, NATO and the international organizations promoted the idea that, albeit with different perspectives, they were working together to help solve Bosnia-Herzegovina's problems. Through the combined briefings, the international community projected an image of cooperation rather than issent and confrontation, which had been prevalent during the UNPROFOR mission. By mid-May 1996, civilian agencies agreed to chair the daily briefing three times a week. All of this served to publicly reinforce NATO's objective of gradually transferring responsibilities to civilian agencies.

The pre-briefing meeting: Fifteen minutes before the daily briefing took place, spokesmen from IFOR and the civilian agencies' spokesmen held a pre-briefing meeting where each discussed what they intended to present at the press conference, and when necessary, asked for additional information. They discussed briefly other events or issues that might arise in questioning. Spokesmen then decided what information to release and in what order. The pre-briefing meeting helped spokesmen to share and compare information. For example, in October 1996, when houses in Mahala, Jusici, and Mostar were destroyed to prevent refugee returns, the UNHCR spokesman and IFOR PI regularly compared notes. This process helped reduce inaccuracies and in some cases, helped de-conflict sensitive issues. It also helped the spokesmen to refrain from publicly criticizing each other and to tone down disagreements. Indicted war criminals was such an area of disagreement. When Alex Ivanko (the UNMIBH spokesman) was asked to make a statement on behalf of the ICTY, he would give advance warning to IFOR at the pre-briefing meeting. Thus IFOR was not caught unprepared and had time to prepare a response.

The Joint Information Coordination Committee (JICC):[114] Every week, IFOR CPIO, ARRC CIO and spokesmen, CJCIMIC chief civil information, the CJIICTF, combat camera, and the major civilian organizations (OHR, UNMIBH, UNHCR, and OSCE) met at the IFOR press center in the Sarajevo Holiday Inn to discuss current activities and future plans. Through the JICC, IFOR PI fostered a strong synergy between those involved in communicating with international and local audiences. This helped de-conflict sensitive issues and promote common strategies. It also provided a forum for international organizations to request support from IFOR. For example, the CJIICTF designed and produced posters and pamphlets for the international organizations. Such requirements were discussed at the JICC (see figure 9: the JICC concept).

---

[114] In planning and for the first few months of IFOR operations, the JICC was an internal coordination forum where ARRC and IFOR PI, the CJIICTF, CJCIMIC, CJ2, and CJ3 coordinated information with operations. When the operational tempo decreased and annex 1A was complied with, CJ2 and CJ3 stopped attending the meeting. In the meantime, IFOR PI had initiated a coordination forum with the major international organizations (OHR, UNHCR, UNMIBH) to coordinate information activities. This meeting was called the Theater Organization Group (TOG), more commonly known within IFOR as "The Other Group". In Spring 1996, when CJ2 and CJ3 stopped attending the JICC, it seemed that the JICC and the TOG served similar purposes. IFOR PI decided to rationalize, invited the civilian organizations to the JICC, and disbanded the TOG. Interview with Capt. Van Dyke, USN, IFOR CPIO, IFOR Headquarters, Sarajevo, 14 October 1997.

Figure 9: The Joint Information Coordination Committee Concept

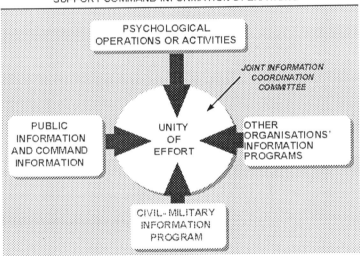

SOURCE: Col. Philips, USA, SHAPE CIMIC Policy

Informal cooperation process: As the combined press conference and coordination meetings developed, informal coordination evolved. Spokesmen called each other to pass information or to seek confirmation and additional details. This process greatly enhanced the information flow between the main agencies working in Bosnia-Herzegovina.

All three divisions failed to reap the benefits that a close coordination with the civilian agencies might have given them. Apart from MND (SW), which tried to establish limited common activities with the civilian organizations (mostly regular briefings with the UNHCR), the other divisions did not seem to seek to coordinate their activities with the local representatives of the civilian organizations operating in their AOR. In MND (N), the force protection rules seriously handicapped the PIO's ability to coordinate with outside organizations. The U.S. PIOs (who led the division's Joint Information Bureau) had to abide by strict force protection rules according to which U.S. forces could only leave the compound in full combat gear and in a four-vehicle convoy. Designed to minimize the risks that the force would face, these rules had a profound impact on the mission of anyone who had to deal with the civil sector.   The PIO could not easily leave the compound. Thus he did not hold regular briefings and had limited interactions with the international organizations' PI staffs. In MND (SE), the PIOs held neither regular coordination meetings nor common activities with the civilian agencies in its AOR. In that case, it seems that strong suspicions about ultimate and ulterior motives remained on both parts.[115] Overall at division level, common activities and coordination forums between PI and the civilian agencies were rare. The coordination at division level slightly increased during the first months of SFOR operations as MND (SE) and MND (SW) multiplied activities in conjunction with the civilian agencies. The author has not been able to assess the validity of the progress made in that specific arena.

National Coordination

IFOR was a 36-nation coalition placed under SACEUR's operational control. As a result, each contingent was expected to report daily to the NATO chain of command. But aside from the NATO chain of command, each nation expected its contingent to report to national authorities. Contingents fulfilled this dual requirement by sending Situation Reports (SITREPs) to IFOR and to their respective MODs. Nations also expected their public officers in theater to follow national guidelines and directives. In a specific case, U.S. public information officers throughout theater were required to participate in a daily teleconference with representatives of the State Department, the Department of Defense, and the National Security Council.[116] However, some

---

[115] Ariane Quentier, UNHCR spokeswoman for Mostar, thought the French (who headed the division) wanted to control her message. Interview with the author, UNHCR headquarters, Sarajevo, 18 October 1997. On the other hand, PIOs working at the division thought that cooperation was only possible if all speakers agreed to a common message. Interview with Maj. Panizzi, ITA, MND (SE) public information officer, MND (SE) headquarters, Mostar, 12 October 1996.

[116] Interview with Col. Icenogle, USA, MND (N) Joint Information Bureau Director, Tuzla, October 1996.

U.S. officers in NATO posts, such as IFOR chief public information officer, did not take part in the daily teleconference because they thought it would undermine their authority within the alliance.

In some cases, national requirements sparked difficulties with IFOR. For example, MND (N) heavily advertised the redeployment of U.S. units out of Bosnia in fall 1996. That line supported the official U.S. position that U.S. troops would leave Bosnia on 20 December 1996, but it contradicted IFOR's effort to keep the redeployment issue in low profile. NATO did not want to incite the factions to act hostilely against IFOR troops at a time when they would be more vulnerable. ARRC had to order the division to stop advertising the redeployment issue.

In other cases, information was formally released to the international press, both by contingents in theater and by home nations, without IFOR's prior knowledge. From interviews with PIOs in theater and at SHAPE, it seems that the issue of casualty announcements sparked the most serious difficulties. According to NATO plans, casualties involving one nation were to be announced by that nation. However, the circumstances of casualties involving one or more nations should be announced by SHAPE. Each nation involved was responsible for releasing personal information, but should have refrained from commenting on the circumstances. In a few instances regarding casualties incidents, nations released information when SHAPE was the formal release authority.[117]

The SFOR/LANDCENT Coordination

Like IFOR, SFOR had established the need for internal and external coordination. However, when LANDCENT assumed theater command in November 1996, the co-operation mechanisms changed dramatically. Most of the mechanisms established by the land component level disappeared when the ARRC left theater in November 1996. Under the LANDCENT/SFOR structure, most of the coordination occurred at COMSFOR staff meetings where the commander gave guidance. Upon arrival in theater, LANDCENT retained or established the following mechanisms, which remained under SFOR.

Internal Coordination

CPIO/COMCJICTF daily meeting: Every morning, SFOR Chief Public Information Officer and the Commander of the CJICTF met to review the operations and incidents of the previous 24 hours and to discuss their activities and responses.

---

[117] For example, an ordnance exploded in a tent, killing and wounding Italian and Portuguese soldiers. In such a case, where two nations were involved in the incident, only NATO had the authority to release information about the circumstances of the incident. In that case, before NATO had released a statement, both nations issued statements describing the incident and placing blame on the other. Interview with LTC Hoehne, USA, SHAPE chief media officer, Mons, 18 December 1996.

COMSFOR Media update: Every morning, SFOR CPIO, the spokesmen, and COMCJICTF attended the COMSFOR media update. With COMSFOR guidance, the PIOs decided what messages to put forward at the daily briefing and how best to handle the day's issues. At the end of the meeting, COMCJICTF presented the planned PSYOP operations for that day. It seems that the meeting was more useful for the PIO than the CJICTF, as COMSFOR did not spend much time discussing the PSYOP effort or giving detailed guidance.[118] The media update continued after Gen. Crouch rotated out of theater and Gen. Shinseki took charge in summer 1997. The author could not assess how successful the meeting was at that point.

LANDCENT Chief Information Officer: In the planning phase, LANDCENT decided that, like the ARRC, it would have a Chief Information Officer (CIO). To that effect, LANDCENT established a two-person Information Operations Cell under CJ3 staff supervision. However, unlike the ARRC, LANDCENT did not provide a clear mission statement for the cell. The CIO, Col. Robey, UKA, was left with defining his own mission. After a few weeks of observation in theater, Col. Robey defined his mission:

> Information Operations seek to achieve sustained support for SFOR and the mandate under which it operates whilst, at the same time, shaping the

---

[118] In spite of this daily meeting, observations conducted in March/April 1997 revealed the CJICTF staff was mostly working with the draft campaign plans as its main source for guidance.

> perceptions of the entities and their leaders in order to achieve an end state compatible with the overall mission objective.[119]

However, during the first six months of SFOR operations, the CIO was never in a position to coordinate effectively the command's information activities. This failure stemmed from a command and control problem. The INFO/OPS cell was placed under CJ3 supervision. However, it sought to coordinate two offices (PI and PSYOP) which had direct access and received direct guidance from COMSFOR. Under such circumstances, it is not surprising that both the CPIO and the COMCJICTF flatly denied any authority to the Chief Information Officer. As Colonel Robey realistically assessed: "I cannot coordinate their work because I have no authority to do so." Not surprisingly, the CIO's attempt to create a new coordination forum essentially failed. In January 1997, the CIO created the Information Coordination Tasking Group (ICTG). The meeting was designed as an internal coordination forum where PIO, PSYOP, civil information, CJ2, and CJ3 convened to determine public information postures and amend them according to unfolding events and/or media and public responses. However, the CPIO and the COMCJICTF sent representatives with no decision-making power, the CJ-9 representative did not work civil information, and the CJ-2 representative did not view it as a worthwhile activity.

---

[119] Interview with Col. Robey, UKA, Chief Information Officer, SFOR Headquarters, Ilidza, 25 March 1997.

External Coordination

Combined Daily Briefing and Pre-Briefing Meeting:
LANDCENT continued the AFSOUTH practice of holding daily briefing and pre-briefing meetings, capitaliz-
ing on IFOR success in that area. Both practices yielded
the same advantages they had during the AFSOUTH
period of IFOR operations. In spring 1997, all participants still considered both activities as worthwhile and
as mutually beneficial as before.[120]

The LANDCENT JICC: LANDCENT decided to continue
holding the JICC meeting to look at mid- to long-term
information activities and policies among the main purveyors of information in theater.[121] However, the meeting seemed to suffer from fading interest. For the first
four months of SFOR operations, the JICC dealt principally with administrative matters (mostly with reorga-
nizing the meeting). In addition, information flow did
not seem to be very effective, as information relevant to
certain staffs or organizations was not mentioned at the
meeting. As a result, attendance to the JICC went down,
even though SFOR PI tried to increase the number of
participants. Many of the primary international organizations (such as UNMIBH, UNHCR, OHR, and OSCE)

---

[120] Interviews conducted with Col. Rausch, USA, SFOR CPIO; Duncan
Bullivan, OHR press and public affairs officer; Alex Ivanko, UNMIBH spokesman;
Betty Dawson, OSCE press and public affairs officer; Kris Janowski, UNHCR
spokesman. All interviews were conducted in Sarajevo, March-April 1997.

[121] The following components participated in the meeting: SFOR CPIO,
SFOR DCPIO, SFOR chief information operations, DCOMCJICTF (or CJICTF S3),
CMTF PAO (invited but did not attend on a regular basis), OHR, UNHCR, UNMIBH,
and OSCE spokesmen.

no longer attended the meeting on a regular basis. Several of their spokesmen did not consider the JICC useful because they already exchanged information at the pre-daily briefing meeting. Among other organizations invited to the JICC (such as UNICEF or the ICRC), many did not have enough staff or did not view the meeting as important enough in terms of their own strategies to show up on a regular basis. In addition, the JICC did not serve the PSYOP requirements well. The civilian organizations' participants to the JICC (IOs' spokesmen) were not the CJICTF's primary points of contact within these organizations. Little coordination between PSYOP and the civilian organizations actually took place at the JICC. For example, during the preparation for the national elections (September 1996), and in spite of the JICC meetings, it became clear that the CJICTF did not have all the information it needed to provide adequate and timely support to the OSCE.[122]

PSYOP LNO to the International Organizations: To overcome these difficulties, IFOR PSYOP assigned an NCO as its liaison officer (LNO) to the international organizations in November 1996. The LNO met and identified points of contact within various civilian organizations, presented PSYOP products and capabilities, gathered information on the civilian organizations' needs and intentions, and detected opportunities for support. When it arrived in theater, the SFOR CJICTF retained the LNO. In addition, two of the task force's officers, the deputy

---

[122] Interview with Maj. Gallo, CJIICTF product development, CJIICTF headquarters, Sarajevo, 22 October 1996.

commander and the chief of product development, also assumed liaison responsibilities (in addition to their primary duties).

The liaison structure helped PSYOP to gain insights into the civilian organizations' work and constraints, and helped the civilian organizations familiarize themselves with PSYOP. However, several shortfalls limited the LNO's effectiveness. First, the liaison officer was given no guidance. Therefore, how to advertise PSYOP to the civilian organization was entirely left to him. This lack of guidance resulted in an unsophisticated and opportunistic approach to support advertising. The CJICTF presented itself as a purveyor of free services (such as cheap printing facility or dissemination tool). By and large, the CJICTF failed to market its expertise (e.g., its ability to develop step-by-step campaigns to achieve attitudinal change). As a result, civilian organizations (with the notable exception of the OSCE which "contracted" its voter education campaign for the municipal elections to a PSYOP personnel) underused the PSYOP capability, asking for help to create one or two products (and not a campaign) or using the task force's resources (such as its printing facility).

Benefits and Difficulties of Cooperation

Cooperation yielded large benefits for both IFOR/SFOR and the international community. The widespread coordination taking place within operational staffs (especially CJ2/CJ3) and with civilian agencies made it possible to develop a synergetic information strategy. It also made it easier to react promptly and comprehensively to significant events as well as the commander's needs.

Benefits

Internal coordination enabled the command to send a unified message, made it less likely that different staffs would develop divergent plans, and facilitated the integration of the information campaign with other tools in the commander's arsenal. During most of IFOR operations, information was always on the commander's mind as one of his potential weapons. CJ3 was aware of the possibility to use the media and PI was aware of ongoing and future operations. Conversely, PIO was always aware of current operations and future plans. In this regard, the creation of a Chief Information Officer (at ARRC level) in December 1995, dedicated to coordinating PSYOP and PI activities on a daily basis, proved beneficial. It made it easier to react promptly to developing situations and to refocus the effort. Some of these benefits, however, were progressively lost when LANDCENT assumed responsibility of operations in November 1996.[123]

External coordination yielded considerable benefits in the field of Public Information. By accounts of civilian and military participants alike, and in comparison with earlier missions, this was perhaps the most extensive

---

[123] See section on "Difficulties," p. 136.

and effective form of civil-military cooperation process for PI in a multinational operation. The daily combined PI activities—

- allowed PIOs working for different organizations with different (if mainly supporting) goals to work together in a climate of trust and confidence;
- enabled PIOs to de-conflict sensitive issues, such as indicted war criminals and destruction of houses to prevent refugee returns;
- allowed for more accurate reporting since the spokesmen exchanged their views and information and checked facts before releasing information at the press briefing; and
- enhanced the flow of information between civilian and military organizations.

The only limitation to this fruitful cooperation was the civilian organizations' reluctance to get fully involved in mid- to long-term planning through the JICC meetings. Indeed, although the major civilian organizations attended the meeting regularly, they did not find it very useful. This shortfall was largely compounded by the strong and effective daily coordination.

Difficulties

While "coordination" is a feel-good concept that almost everyone agrees on, the reality is that it is not easy to implement. In the field of internal coordination, IFOR and SFOR experiences showed that effective coordination not only depends on institutionalized mechanisms and forums, but also relies heavily on the commander's commitment. Even the best coordination mechanisms will not work unless the participants are willing for them to work. With relatively similar internal mechanisms, AFSOUTH/ARRC and LANDCENT did not achieve a similar degree of coordination. During the first nine months of SFOR operations, closeness with the commander seemed to progressively recede.[124] In a headquarters with 23 general officers, the CPIO and COMCJICTF (both O-6s) had difficulty competing for COMSFOR's attention. The informal relations between PI/PSYOP and the commanding general all but disappeared; encounters became mostly limited to the formal morning meetings.

Without the commander's support, the level of internal coordination decayed, PI and PSYOP integration with the command group diminished, and PI and PSYOP knowledge of future plans seemed to recede. In fact, PI and PSYOP seemed to be relegated to more of a support activity than a key non-lethal weapon in the commander's arsenal. This diminished access did not keep the PI and CJICTF in the loop and limited their ability to contribute effectively to mission accomplishment. This became clear in July 1997, when SFOR troops staged raids to capture two Bosnian Serb indicted war criminals. However, for an operation which would be sensitive to the Bosnian Serb population and would affect SFOR's image throughout the AOR (and interna-

---

[124] This problem was observed and analyzed during the first nine months of SFOR operations, until SFOR seized TV transmitters across Republika Srpska in October 1997.

tionally), neither the chief PIO nor the commander of the CJICTF were brought into the planning in a timely fashion. As a result, the RS press, not SFOR, set the agenda. The PI/CJICTF could not act proactively, but were forced to respond to a series of accusations launched in the RS press.[125] Likewise, when SFOR seized TV transmitters in Republika Srpska (September-October 1997), the CJICTF was apparently not closely linked with planning and was caught unprepared to deal with the consequences of the seizures.[126]

IFOR/SFOR's experience with external coordination also revealed some difficulties. Cooperation requires compromise, a give-and-take process with benefits and costs. Early in *Joint Endeavour*, IFOR leadership decided that coordination with the civilian agencies was necessary to enhance the operation's credibility. How-

---

[125] On 10 July 1997, British troops conducted two commando operations to arrest two indicted war criminals in Republika Srpska. The UK soldiers killed one in self-defense, and detained the other one. NATO turned him over to the ICTY to stand trial. The COMCJICTF was brought into the planning too days before the raid and was not allowed to involve his staff in the planning. As a result, no products were ready for dissemination to explain why and how the two men had been arrested. Apparently, the CPIO learnt of the operation after it was underway. Almost immediately, the Bosnian Serb media unleashed a violent anti-NATO propaganda, distorting the facts and calling for retaliation against NATO troops. The PI/CJICTF were poorly prepared to respond to these attacks. There are good reasons to restrict the number of personnel with knowledge of this type of commando-operations, if only because they rely heavily on the ability to surprise the adversary. But leaving the Chief PIO and PSYOP Commander among the uninformed had a direct, immediate and inescapable consequence: it decreased COMSFOR's ability to explain and justify the operation to the locals. Meanwhile, COMSFOR and SACEUR agreed at that stage that there were significant problems with the PSYOP campaign and ordered an assessment mission. This U.S. assessment mission took place in August 1997.

[126] According to newspaper accounts, internal coordination seemed to have improved when Dutch troops arrested two Bosnian Croat indicted war criminals on 18 December 1997. As soon as the raid occurred, the Bosnian Croat radio broadcasted a NATO message urging the population to remain calm. See Colin Soloway, "Dutch Troops Capture 2 Croat War Criminal Suspects," *The Washington Post*, 19 December 1997, A43.

ever, civilian agencies were first reluctant to cooperate with IFOR out of fear of losing their freedom of speech. As operations unfolded, civilian organizations came to realize that they would benefit from coordination. As a result, they made concessions to de-conflict sensitive issues with IFOR and avoid direct public criticisms of IFOR operations. IFOR, on the other hand, bore the financial cost of the deal by paying for the Holiday Inn rental and providing manpower and equipment for the press center. In general terms, this experience shows two things. Partners have to recognize the benefits and costs of coordination. Such realization requires understanding of partner organizations to define the possibilities and arouse desire to execute coordination. It was in this realm of "understanding" that coordination amongst the international elements in Bosnia faced perhaps its greatest challenge. Second, the process of understanding and recognizing can take time and delay implementation of full coordination. In the case of IFOR, it took five months before full coordination between the PI, PSYOP, civil information, and civilian organization was fully in place.

External coordination in the PSYOP field was a particularly challenging task and did not flow as smoothly as that in the PI arena. Traditionally, PSYOP elements do not operate closely with civilian organizations. During *Joint Endeavour* and *Joint Guard*, supporting civilian agencies constituted a major part of the PSYOP effort. However, throughout the operations, the PSYOP/civilian organizations interface did not form an effective basis for communicating requirements and capabilities between organizations. Civilian organizations had difficulties formulating clear requirements to the PSYOP task force. Conversely, the PSYOP task force did not always understand the civilian organizations' requirements and the constraints they were operating under. Many of these problems can be related to the above-mentioned requirement for understanding: it is not necessarily that any of those involved (military or civilian) were not, in the end, willing to coordinate or cooperate, but that they lacked sufficient understanding of the other organization to work effectively together. Such incomprehension can only be detrimental to the overall effort.

Conclusion

When implemented, internal and external coordination operated as force multipliers for NATO commanders in Bosnia. During IFOR operations, in particular, internal coordination enabled the commander to use PI and PSYOP effectively to communicate with various audiences. External coordination, especially in the PI field, allowed the international community to develop synergetic information strategies among the main players in DPA implementation. Although coordination proved beneficial, it was difficult to achieve. The IFOR experience showed that external coordination is a give-and-take process which requires compromise, while the SFOR experience showed that successful internal coordination depends on the commander's commitment.

Chapter 6:
Assessing Information
Activities in Bosnia

Operations *Joint Endeavour* (December 1995-December 1996) and *Joint Guard* (December 1996 on) revealed the critical nature of information activities in peace operations as the principal means of communication between NATO commanders and various audiences. The overall campaign contributed to mission accomplishment by facilitating communication with the factions and helping maintain public opinion support. However, obstacles and challenges limited the campaign's contribution to mission accomplishment. This chapter assesses the successes and limits of NATO information activities in Bosnia-Herzegovina.

Successes

The Public Information Campaign

The information campaign's primary contribution to mission accomplishment lay in the continued support for or neutrality toward NATO-led operations in the contributing nations. Throughout operations, international and national public opinions showed either support or neutrality toward the mission. No major political controversy emerged at government level (between the executive and legislative bodies, or between the government and political activists) during the accomplishment of IFOR mission. More importantly, a smooth transition from IFOR to an 18-month SFOR mission took place without much difficulties. A simplistic view could credit NATO public information for such success, if only because public information was tasked with gaining and maintaining public support. In fact, it is difficult to assert any direct, single causality link.[127] However, it seems likely that the IFOR/SFOR public information campaign contributed to this end result along with other operational elements, such as low casualties and a progressive return to normalcy.

The information campaign was based upon principles that served both the commanders and the international public's needs. By providing complete, timely, and ac-

---

[127] In fact, studies on the collapse of public opinion support for military operations have identified two major causes of collapse: the rise of casualties and lack of presidential leadership. See Eric V. Larson, *Casualties and Consensus: The Historical Role of Casualties in Domestic Support for U.S. Military Operations*, Santa Monica, CA, RAND publication, 1996.

curate information, the PIO established its credibility with the international and national media. By establishing credibility with reporters, IFOR/SFOR PI thus reduced the likelihood of unjustified negative stories and gave IFOR/SFOR a better chance to have their side of the story heard. On the media side, reporters publicly expressed their satisfaction with the arrangements made throughout the operations.[128] For most of IFOR/SFOR operations, several internal arrangements adequately supported the requirement for dissemination of complete, timely, and accurate information:

- Allowing a functional chain of information linking PI officers throughout theater proved beneficial. It sped up information flow and allowed PI to provide the media with timely information.
- Appropriate delegation of release of authority to the theater force commander (or whomever he decided to delegate his authority to).
- Close integration with operational staffs and close relationships with commanders.

PI/PSYOP Integration Within the Command Group

The close integration of IFOR PI and PSYOP within the command group also contributed to mission accomplishment. This enabled PI and PSYOP to be more effective

---

[128] For example, Nik Gowing (BBC TV) and Kurt Schork (Reuters) publicly praised IFOR efforts to provide relevant information in a timely fashion. Rémy Ourdan, reporter for the French daily Le Monde, considered that IFOR had been forthcoming with its operations. A New York Times reporter commented that JOINT ENDEAVOUR was the "best military-media relationship he had ever seen."

tools in the commander's arsenal. Until the transition with LANDCENT (November 1996), PI and PSYOP had close interactions with operational staffs, in particular CJ3. Both PI and PSYOP were kept informed of current operations and future plans. CJ3 was aware of the possibility to use PI and PSYOP as part of operations. CJ3 was also in a position to learn information from PI and PSYOP. In addition, PI and PSYOP were aware of ongoing and future operations. Such interaction allowed PI and PSYOP to better prepare for contingencies. Seemingly, the close relationship between PI, PSYOP, and COMIFOR/COMARRC allowed the CPIO and COMCJIICTF to understand their commanders' wishes and thinking. This close relationship allowed them to work in a climate of mutual trust and confidence which benefited everyone and enhanced the mission. The close relationship eroded after LANDCENT assumed command of the operation. From then on, closeness with commanders receded and integration with other operational staffs loosened. PI and PSYOP knowledge of future plans diminished, as illustrated by the July 1997 raid against indicted war criminals (discussed earlier). On that occasion, SFOR could not effectively use information as a non-lethal weapons since neither the PIO nor the CJICTF were integrated into the operational planning.

Information as a Non-Lethal Weapon

Another important contribution to mission accomplishment was the use of information to enforce the FWF's compliance with the DPA provisions, deter violence, and resolve crisis. In a peace support operation, where the outside force does not conduct combat operations, the commander has to place a greater reliance on non-lethal weapons. While every unit has some capability in this realm, PI and PSYOP are two critical non-lethal weapons. Throughout the operation, commanders made extensive use of public information and PSYOP to help achieve operational goals and relied on information assets (mostly PI and PSYOP) to influence the FWF's behaviors in case of crisis. Adequate information flow and close coordination between staff components allowed the commander to effectively use PI and PSYOP as a non-lethal weapon. It was one of the commander's major tools to communicate intentions, might, and resolve to the local populations and the FWF.

On a routine basis, public information was used to reinforce the appropriateness of IFOR's actions. For example, the MND (SW) commander used his media operations to publicly lay blame on the factions for not fully complying with annex 1A of the DPA.[129] In a number of high-profile incidents, IFOR/SFOR and/or the international organizations used public announcements to place pressure on the FWF to enforce compliance with their decisions. For example, in summer 1996, the Bosnian Serb chief of police in Prijedor fired a warning shot at IFOR troops challenging him about unauthorized weapons. In response, COMIFOR approved an information plan designed to apply gradual pressure on the RS leaders to oust the Prijedor chief of police and

---

[129] Interview with LTC Paul Brook, UKA, Chief Media Operations, MND (SW), Banja Luka, October 1996.

hand over the unauthorized weapons. Meanwhile, COMARRC developed contingency plans to enforce IFOR's objective (ousting the chief police) if necessary. As international pressure mounted, the RS turned over the weapons and designated a new police chief.[130] In another case, in March 1997, the Office of the High Representative and the UNMIBH combined their efforts to get the Mostar authorities to remove road bumps they had placed that impeded the Bosniacs' freedom of movement in town. After repeated demands to remove the bumps and under the threat of sanctions, the Bosnian Croats complied.

However, information activities are a double-edged sword as they can produce unexpected results. In spring 1996, RS leaders refused to let IFOR troops check an ammunition depot in Han Pijesak. COMIFOR then decided to have his spokesman announce at the daily briefing that IFOR recommended all IOs/NGOs pull out of Republika Srpska, as IFOR was about to use force to support the depot inspection, and they could be at risk for retaliation. After a few days, the RS accepted IFOR's ultimatum and opened the depot for inspection.[131] However, the NGO community was probably more surprised at IFOR's announcement than the RS leaders. Soon after the public announcement, NGO personnel in the RS anxiously called their headquarters back on the Federation side, asking for instructions. Unaware of IFOR's decisions, the IOs were unable to provide any

---

[130] Interview with Capt. Van Dyke, USN, IFOR CPIO from December 1995 to November 1996, Sarajevo, 17 October 1996.

[131] Interview with Col. Serveille, FRA, IFOR DCPIO from July to December 1996, Sarajevo, 18 October 1996.

guidance to their operatives in Republika Srpska. This deceptive announcement generated a great deal of mistrust between IFOR and the IO/NGO community.

Coordination with International Organizations

Another important contribution of information activities to mission accomplishment was the fruitful coordination established with international organizations, in particular in the field of public information. Combined activities between IFOR/SFOR, OHR, UNHCR, OSCE, and UNMIBH spokesmen were mutually beneficial at different levels. By accounts of civilian and military participants alike, and in comparison with earlier missions, this was perhaps the most extensive and effective civilian-military cooperation process for PI in a multinational operation. These combined activities symbolized the international community's unity on behalf of peace and reconstruction in B-H. With the daily combined briefings, the international community sought to present itself as united in a common effort in support of DPA implementation. The participants did not pretend to agree on every issue.[132] But by agreeing to brief together, the international organizations promoted the idea that, albeit with different perspectives, they were all working together on behalf of Bosnia-Herzegovina. This was an important achievement as the UNPROFOR pe-

---

[132] Hence, they did not. For a long time, the most divisive issue concerned SFOR's role in arresting indicted war criminals. Civilian organizations (such as the OHR or the UN) argued that IFOR/SFOR was the only force in Bosnia capable of arresting the war criminals. IFOR, then SFOR long maintained that only a police force should get involved in tracking down criminals. Other divisive issues included the role of IFOR/SFOR in curbing civil disorders and the role of IFOR/SFOR in enforcing refugee returns.

riod had been marked with dissent, contradictions, and antagonism between the military force (blue berets) and civilian agencies (such as the UNHCR). Combined daily activities also enhanced the information flow between military and civilian organizations. As far as the author is aware, the daily combined PI activities represented the most frequent, most senior daily interplay between IFOR/SFOR and the civilian agencies across the operation.[133] Much of the credit for this success lies on the PI shoulders, as COMIFOR Chief Public Information Officer and COMARRC Chief Information Officer initiated widespread cooperation with other operational elements and with international organizations.

Although links between the PSYOP and the international organizations were established, they met numerous obstacles. Mutual unfamiliarity between psychological operations and civilian agencies and lack of appropriate structures to communicate requirements complicated the cooperation. Nevertheless, the PSYOP/ international organizations coordination helped familiarize international organizations with PSYOP and contributed to the climate of cooperation between civilian and military organizations. PSYOP support to international organizations also enhanced the international or-

---

[133] This is an important element for CIMIC issues. Current doctrine (either NATO or US) does not consider Public Information as an important element of liaison and coordination between a military force and civilian organizations. It is in fact, likely, that such PIOs meetings would represent the most frequent senior level interaction between organizations. This was certainly the case in Bosnia-Herzegovina where PIOs met more frequently than the Principals' meetings (a regular meeting between COMIFOR/COMSFOR and the leaders of the civilian organizations). As was the case with IFOR/ARRC/SFOR PIOs, the civilian organization spokesmen had direct and frequent access to the organizations' heads and thus were very senior staffs, in practice, if not title.

ganizations' information campaigns. In particular, the PSYOP support enabled the OSCE to run far-reaching campaigns to educate voters on the importance of elections and inform them on the rules and regulations governing the electoral process. According to Diana Cepeda, Director of OSCE voter education program for the municipal election voter registration campaign, "SFOR support has enabled the OSCE to prepare a better quality campaign. We could have done something without SFOR support, but it would not have been as good as what we have finally put out."[134] The PSYOP support was also valuable to other organizations, such as the UN Mine Action Center (UNMAC). Hopefully, the Bosnia experience paved the way for a new form of cooperation in future peace support operations.

Limits

The major limit to NATO information activities from December 1995 to fall 1997 lay in its limited effectiveness to offer the local populations a credible alternative view of the international community's efforts to that presented by the factions and to counter local propaganda and disinformation.

---

[134] Interview with Diana Cepada, OSCE voter education director, OSCE headquarters, Sarajevo, 8 April 1997.

The Limited Promotion of NATO's Message

Throughout the operation NATO experienced difficulties in communicating effectively with local audiences.[135] Neither the PIO nor the PSYOP task force were fully adapted to communicate with Bosnian audiences. The original PI planning and initial execution, for example, did not provide for the requirements of local reporters. As PI sought to promote international understanding for the mission, it did not place a high priority on fostering good relations with local journalists. Initially, although NATO PI opportunities were open to local journalists, IFOR made few efforts to accommodate the specific needs of the local press. Reporters from the various entities reluctantly traveled to other entities' territory to attend IFOR/SFOR press conferences. This restriction limited the local journalists' exposure to NATO's message. IFOR PI first and foremost tried to meet the international press corps' agenda.[136] IFOR PI developed into a belief that the local media were critical but did not believe they had much impact with local journalists. IFOR, but mostly SFOR, tried to design specific activi-

---

[135] NATO is not the first international organization to experience difficulties communicating with the local population in Bosnia. During the war, the International Committee of the Red Cross faced grave difficulties to ascertain its humanitarian, neutral status amidst the propaganda war that the factions had launched. See Michèle Mercier, *Crimes without punishment: Humanitarian Action in Former Yugoslavia*, Chapter 6: "On the proper use of propaganda," London, Pluto Press, 1995.

[136] Colonel Mulvey, USA, who replaced Captain Van Dyke as IFOR Chief PIO in November 1996, expressed surprise at how the international and local journalists were interested in vastly different stories. He noted that international journalists were more interested in the fate of Dayton, the follow-on force, whereas the locals (which expected a follow-on force) wanted information on economic reconstruction and civil-military cooperation. Conversation with Col. Mulvey, USA, LANDCENT CPIO, IFOR CPIC, Sarajevo, 23 October 1996.

ties targeted at the local media. In particular, SFOR arranged two press conferences a week in RS territory. It also arranged to have a weekly press conference in Serbo-Croat at the Holiday Inn. However, these efforts were never deemed as important or received significant focus as dealing with international journalists. The CJICTF, on the other hand, was not well-equipped to communicate effectively with a "first-world" audience such as the Bosnian population. As explained in more detail in chapter 3, the PSYOP task forces did not have adequate equipment to compete with established media. In particular, the CJICTF did not have a TV capability in a country where an overwhelming majority of people get their news from the local television.

Second, the nature of the IFOR/SFOR message reduced its potential impact. In general, the PSYOP messages were based on general principles (such as "elections will decide your future" or "reconciliation is good") and shied away from difficult issues. For example, the campaign never addressed the fact that the FWF were hindering Dayton Agreement implementation. The campaign also failed to tackle controversial topics such as indicted war criminals out of fear that it could lead to resentment and hostility against NATO troops. Occasionally, the PIO message was direct and aggressive, but only when the factions failed to comply with annex 1A of the Dayton Peace Agreement or threatened NATO troops. On issues other than annex 1A, IFOR and SFOR PI kept a rather low profile. NATO rarely used information activities to pressure the FWF into compliance. On these issues, IFOR and SFOR PI

usually let the civilian organizations deliver hard messages, avoided pointing fingers, and restricted themselves to factual and non-controversial issues.

Overall, several contradictions limited the effectiveness
of NATO's message. NATO could not always follow up
a message with relevant action, so there was no positive reinforcement to enhance the credibility of the message. For example, throughout much of 1996, NATO
ran a campaign supporting freedom of movement. However, NATO would not and could not guarantee that
Bosnians crossing the IEBL into the territory of another
ethnic group would be safe. For all practical purposes,
the few who undertook such a journey put themselves
at risk. The NATO campaign did not lead to significant
behavioral change among the Bosnians because NATO
could not guarantee safety. Second, NATO avoided tar-
geting leaders. This approach did not allow condemna-
tion of the political tricks that the factions' employed to
block the peace process. Third, NATO chose not to attack some of the mythologies that block the peace process. For example, NATO has not taken apart the myth
that only radical Serbs can protect the Serbs and that
the international community is behind some kind of plot
to eliminate the Serb people. NATO and the PSYOP
campaign allowed themselves to be cornered in a situation with few viable options. Most public actions
seemed to punish the Serbs for failing to cooperate.[137]
In the meantime, the few "good news" items (such as

---

[137] For example in 1996, the Republika Srpska received less than 3 percent
of the total aid to Bosnia-Herzegovina because its authorities failed to cooperate on
the issue of common institutions.

successful minority returns) could not be publicized for fear they might trigger a hostile reaction. Almost no matter the situation, the Bosnian Serb media depicted NATO as some type of evil entity.

Fighting Disinformation

Most of all, neither IFOR/SFOR PI nor the CJICTF was able to fight the factions' disinformation attempts. Confronting disinformation is a difficult problem in the delicate political environment of a peace operation. Through fall 1997, NATO had not adequately answered the challenge of how to respond to dishonest and manipulative factional reporting. In fact, responding to the parties' disinformation seemed to be beyond capabilities and certainly outside perceived mandates. However, disinformation was thriving across theater. In March 1996, the Pale media launched a campaign encouraging the Bosnian Serbs living in the Sarajevo suburbs to be transferred to the Bosniac authorities to flee. Pale TV argued that Bosnian Serb safety could no longer be guaranteed after the transfer of authority. Later that same year, the Bosniac press reported that the French buried nuclear waste on Mount Ingman. Neither NATO nor French authorities responded because they became aware of the disinformation well after a chance for a timely response.[138] More recently, after SFOR special operations forces arrested Bosnian Serb indicted war criminals on 10 July 1997, Bosnian Serb TV (controlled by a faction loyal to Radovan Karadzic) launched a viru-

---

[138] Interview with Pierre Servent, media relation advisor to the French Minister of Defense, Paris, November 1996.

lent anti-NATO campaign comparing SFOR troops to the Nazis.[139] Subsequently, when SFOR CIMIC announced that railways between Tuzla and Brcko would be repaired by an Italian brigade, the Bosnian Serb television argued it was designed to transport war criminals to The Hague.

Fighting disinformation properly would have required interaction between all staffs in charge of information activities (such as PI and PSYOP) and CJ2 (intelligence). Such coordination did not seem to take place in Bosnia, at least at SFOR HQ.[140] PI and intelligence staffs had little formal background on which to develop a fruitful relationship.[141] In addition, public information officers view close ties to the intelligence community as a threat to credibility with journalists. On the other side, intelligence staffs seem almost oblivious of the PI arena. Built on such a background, it should not be surprising that there was only a tenuous relationship between the CJ2 and PIOs in Bosnia. In the field of PSYOP, the need for a relationship with intelligence is well-established. In combat operations, PSYOP is a primary consumer of intelligence, as it needs intelligence inputs to design and time its campaigns. In peace support operations, PSYOP is as much a provider of intelligence as a con-

---

[139] Jeffrey Fleishman, "Propaganda Fuels Serbs' Hatred: Struggle Puts NATO Forces in the Middle," *The Philadelphia Inquirer*, 23 September 1997, p 3.

[140] The author mostly studied this relationship during SFOR operations. These findings do not necessarily apply to IFOR.

[141] Neither the NATO Public Information nor the intelligence doctrines discuss any connection between public information and intelligence.

sumer.   But under SFOR, the CJICTF/intelligence interface was weak, as neither the CJICTF nor the CJ2
seemed to place a high priority on the PSYOP/intel link.

Perhaps because of these weak links, as of spring 1997,
no HQ SFOR element tracked disinformation attempts.
As far as the author is aware, within the NATO organization, only the SFOR CIO tried to understand factional
disinformation attempts.   However, he did not have an
adequate structure to maintain and analyze a meaningful, comprehensive database. In addition, neither PI
nor the CJICTF commanders and staffs campaign
thought they should engage in countering disinformation.

A Lack of Vision

In fact, NATO's information strategy was plagued from
the start by a lack of vision. With IFOR and SFOR, the
NAC did not clarify the mission's end state, but instead
relied on two arbitrary, barely believed end dates (12
months in IFOR's case, and 18 months in SFOR's case)
to define the mission's final objective.[142] In December
1995, the NAC defined IFOR's mission as enforcing the
cessation of hostilities for 12 months.   In December
1996, the NAC defined SFOR's mission as enforcing
the cessation of hostilities for an additional 18-month
period. Such definitions were first and foremost meant
to reassure the contributing nations' legislatures and
public opinion, especially in the United States, that their

---

[142] An end state establishes the set of conditions that an operation seeks to
achieve. Such conditions should allow force withdrawal. An end date establishes a
time certain for ending the operation regardless of the situation on the ground.

troops would not be committed to an open-ended operation. Within the United States at least, the spectrum
of Vietnam hangs over such definitions. However, using end dates rather than an end state did not provide
an articulated vision of what NATO sought to achieve in
Bosnia and of the conditions that would make a departure of NATO forces possible without a resumption of
hostilities between the factions.

This absence of a clear end state hampered both the
IFOR and SFOR PSYOP campaigns. Without a clear
end state, the PSYOP campaign could not formulate a
step-by-step campaign toward a clear objective. During IFOR operations, all information activities were
geared toward one goal: NATO is here for one year to
enforce the cessation of hostilities so the factions can
work their differences out. For that year, NATO will use
any necessary measure to enforce its mandate, and
the factions and civilian organizations have the responsibility to resolve policy issues. This guideline gave the
information campaign a direction to work toward. IFOR
information campaigns thus mostly focused on force
protection issues and NATO might and resolve, and promoted civilian implementation of the DPA. These campaigns successfully conveyed the message that NATO
would not tolerate any attack or obstacles to its mission. However, these campaigns did little to help set
the conditions for a viable withdrawal of NATO forces.

Right from the start of SFOR's mission, several factors
almost immediately prevented the PSYOP campaign
from relying on the artificial deadline (June 1998) as its

objective. First, several NATO nations hinted that there should be a follow-on force.[143] Second, the Clinton administration ventured to seek support for such an operation and in December 1997 announced an intention to extend U.S. commitment to Bosnia.[144] Finally, NATO's policy toward DPA implementation progressively evolved. In spring 1997, HQ SFOR began exploring a more aggressive approach to DPA implementation and began to work more closely with the international organizations. However, as these changes occurred, no articulated vision had replaced the deadline fantasy and had been articulated to the PSYOP force. As a result, PSYOP personnel did not seem to have a clear understanding of what their mission was and felt they were conducting a wide range of operations without understanding how they contributed to mission accomplishment. Effective PSYOP in Bosnia requires that the CJICTF be given a clear vision of what needs to be achieved.

Learning From Experience?

The Transmitters War

Eventually, the information campaign's inadequacies came to light and the international community decided to pay more attention to the issue of media democrati-

---

[143] Effie Hathen, "Cohen says pullout by NATO set, too," *European Stars and Stripes*, 6 March 1997, p 1; Fredrik Dahl, "Clinton urged to extend mission in Bosnia: Otherwise European Allies won't stay," *The Washington Times*, 16 September 1997, p 12.

[144] Richard C. Gross, "Expect U.S. to stay in Bosnia," *The Washington Times*, 28 September 1997, p 8; Richard C. Gross, "Holbrooke strongly hints at longer stint in Bosnia," *The Washington Times*, 9 October 1997, p 13.

zation and use of the media to foster the factions' political goals. In May 1997, at the Sintra meeting, the Peace Implementation Council (PIC) tasked the Office of the High Representative with monitoring and sanctioning local media.[145] Although it provided no details on how to do so, the PIC tasked the OHR to enforce democratic and professional media standards. No international institution had had such power in Bosnia until then. Meanwhile, two events gave SFOR a window of opportunity to also strengthen its attitude in that regard. First, the operation to detain two indicted war criminals in Prijedor (Simo Drljaca and Milan Kovacevic) in early July triggered an angry media campaign by Bosnian Serb media. In particular, SRT portrayed the operation as one more example of the international community's plot to destroy the Serb people. The campaign heated up when SFOR undertook, in conjunction with the IPTF, searches of RS police stations (in Banja Luka and Brcko) in late summer. SRT drew analogies between the World War II Nazi occupation and the SFOR mission and called for Bosnian Serbs to resist NATO operations.[146] Sec-

---

[145] In 1996, the OSCE was tasked with monitoring the content of local media reporting and examining complaints about local coverage. Under its mandate, the OSCE could impose sanctions on media outlets who used inflammatory and hate speech and who did not allow alternative viewpoints. However, the OSCE had limited power to enforce its decisions. For example, during the national elections campaign, the OSCE examined 40 complaints for inflammatory language and defamation and issued letters of warning. However, the process did not significantly alter the local media behaviors. For a critical review of the OSCE charter, see Christine Spolar, "Watch on Media Blinks in Bosnia," *The Washington Post*, 6 August 1996, p 12; and Jonathan C. Randal, "Demands Scaled Back for Free Press in Bosnia as Prerequisite for Vote," *The Washington Post*, 12 June 1996, p 25.

[146] Such calls gave SFOR the legal argument needed to take action against SRT, because they incited violence against NATO troops. Therefore, hostile actions against SRT were justified by the need to protect troops. This incident was not the first time local media had launched a hate campaign against the international community. For example, in September 1996, local media and television in Zvornik (Republika Srpska) launched a hate campaign against the international police task force (IPTF) after it intervened in support of Muslim refugees attempting to return to

ond, the power struggle in RS between Momcilo Krajisnik (pro-Karadzic) and RS president Biljana Plavsic expanded the international community's options to deal with the crisis. The power struggle unexpectedly heated up in early summer 1997 when Plavsic decided to dissolve the RS parliament and called for new elections in November 1997. The struggle caused a split within the RS state television, with journalists and editors from the Banja Luka studio deciding to split away from Pale direction after Pale manipulated a broadcast on SFOR searches in police stations.

SFOR and OHR tried to exploit these developments to their advantage. First, SFOR and OHR encouraged SRT Pale to tone down its anti-Dayton, anti-NATO rhetoric with a package of "carrots and sticks." The OHR negotiated an agreement whereby SRT Pale agreed to stop its anti-NATO campaign and air programs on the DPA sponsored by the international community. In exchange, they would remain open. The sticks came in the form of threats of military action if SRT Pale did not comply. In late September, Belgrade brokered an agreement between Momcilo Krajisnik and Bijlana Plavsic, according to which SRT Pale and SRT Banja Luka would broadcast each others' work on alternate days. For some days, the agreement was honored and both stations toned down their commentaries. However, after SRT Pale heavily edited a tape on the ICTY mission, SFOR

---

nearby Mahala. See Sue Palumbo, "Radio, TV rant at task force," *The European Stars and Stripes*, 4 September 1996, p 6.

seized four transmitters in eastern Bosnia, thus reducing considerably the SRT Pale footprint.[147] At this stage, SRT loyal to Bijlana Plavsic broadcasts across the RS.

The Light at the End of the Tunnel?

Taking down the SDS transmitters and handing them over to Bijlana Plavsic had two benefits. The operation enabled the international community to shut down the most extremist anti-NATO, anti-Dayton propaganda in RS from the largest medium in the country—television. The operation subsequently allowed the international community to increase the visibility of its message in Republika Srpska. But these benefits came at a cost. First, the international community decided to arbitrarily shut down a voice in RS when it had been sponsoring freedom of speech for the past two years. It thus found itself in the awkward position of defending curbing the very notion it promoted: freedom of speech and press.[148] Second, there were substantial shortcomings in the planning and execution of these operations which revealed a lack of preparation and vision as to why these operations were taking place. For example, the agreement to broadcast one hour of internationally sponsored

---

[147] For a detailed chronology of the transmitters war, see Marina Bowder, "The Transmitter War," *War Report: Bulletin of the institute of war and peace reporting*, October 1997, no 55, p 41-42; Lee Hockstader, "Bosnian Serbs Back Off, but Get TV Tower," *The Washington Post*, 3 September 1997, p 21; "U.S. orders three electronic warfare warplanes to Bosnia," *The Baltimore Sun*, 12 September 1997, p 21; Elisabeth Neuffer, "Media war in Bosnia gives Serbs a choice for truth," *The Boston Globe*, 22 September 1997, p 1; Mike O'Connor, "NATO Troops Shut Down Bosnian Serb TV Network," *The New York Times*, 21 October 1997.

[148] For a brief summary of the pros and cons, see letter to the editor by Morton I. Abramowitz and Ayeh Neier, "Bosnian Serb Media are Threat to Dayton," *The New York Times*, 12 September 1997.

program was negotiated without a clear view of how this hour of daily programming would be produced. As a result, SFOR CJICTF was tasked with filling in although it does not have the equipment or resources to produce like a network. In another example, the operation to seize the four transmitters in eastern Bosnia was planned without the PSYOP support. So, after SFOR shut down the transmissions, it had to improvise some actions to explain to the Bosnian Serbs why they were receiving snow on their television sets. A better integration of PSYOP in the planning process would have anticipated this problem and led to a better response.

Finally, taking down SRT Pale transmitters was no panacea. In the new RS media landscape, most broadcast media now back Bijlana Plavsic. Although she has, admittedly, agreed to cooperate with the international community to implement the Dayton Peace Agreement, Plavsic is still a proud representative of Serb nationalism. Her new party, the SNS, is populated with former SDS dignitaries who back the SDS program.[149] Across the country, in spite of the international community's efforts, most local media continue to act as tools of their respective factions.[150] Since early in the war, Bosnia-Herzegovina media were divided along ethnic lines:

---

[149] For a detailed view of the differences and common points between the SDS and the SNS, see "Ostoja Knezevic: Changing Sides," *WarReport*, October 1997, no 55, p 31.

[150] For additional information on the status of the press within the region, see Kati Morton, "Key to the Balkans: A Free Press," *The Washington Post*, 31 May 1996, p 23; Mark M. Nelson, "Biting the Hand: Zagreb Radio 101 Gave Him His Political Start: In Charge, He Hates It," *The Wall Street Journal*, 25 July 1996, p 1; Frangoise J. Hampson, "Incitement and the Media Responsibility of and for the Media in the Conflicts in the Former Yugoslavia," *Papers in the Theory and Practice of Human Rights*, The Human Rights Center, University of Essex, UK, 1993.

Bosniacs, Bosnian Serbs, and Bosnian Croats. Throughout the war, local media zealously passed along their faction's propaganda and disinformation.   As a result, the factions strictly controlled editorial content. In spite of the international community's efforts, this state of affairs did not stop after Dayton. Local media are still closely tied to the factions and their interests.[151] They spread disinformation as they see fit their factions' political objectives. They gave little to no time/space to opposition parties or alternate viewpoints to the official one. The factions also commonly used the media to justify their actions (and more often their non-actions) in implementing the DPA, while swearing that they are willing to make peace. As such, a majority of the local media very much remain a tool in the hands of the dominating parties in their continuing struggle for national identity. By and large, local media still contribute to the factions' strategy of undermining the Dayton agreement. Everyday reporting provides ample proof of their allegiance to the FWF.[152]

---

[151] Divisions PIOs during IFOR and SFOR operations encountered many situations where their efforts to provide information resulted in distorted reporting that fitted the factions' interests. For example, in Summer 1996 in MND (SE), the Spanish Brigade announced its civil engineers would solidify a mobile bridge and donate it to the city of Mostar. The brigade commander explained that a bridge over the Neretva (the river flowing through Mostar) would be a powerful symbol of reconciliation. All local media felt otherwise, spread all kinds of rumors and finally accused the Spanish brigade of having caused damages to the structure. Major Marconnet, the division's PIO, explained: "It is very difficult to get a fair shot with the local media. We give them information on our activities, encourage them to cover what we do, but they will put a spin on it, a spin that fit their factions' political agenda." Interview with the author, MND (SE) headquarters, Mostar, October 1996.

[152] Examples of their allegiance to the FWF include the following: through Fall 1996, a series of attempted refugee returns in the Zone of Separation sparked incidents between the Bosniac refugees (who wanted to return) and RS mobs and authorities (who sought to prevent them). Bosniac media supported the returnees (without acknowledging that they were manipulated by the Bosniac government to repossess territory in the RS) and criticized the international community for not enforcing the returns. Meanwhile, the Bosnian Serb media portrayed the returns as unlawful and as an endangerment to the Serb nation. More generally, most Bosniac

The degree to which the local media are still under the factions' control is worrisome because most Bosnians get their news from and trust most these outlets. According to a poll conducted by the U.S. Information Agency in Bosnia in July 1997, Bosnians tend to rely mostly on "media sources which are closely aligned with parties and/or strongly influenced by regional authorities more than any other."[153] Bosniacs mostly rely on the pro-government or party-controlled media sources. Bosnian Serbs mostly rely on SRT and Serbian sources from Belgrade (the poll was taken before the break-up of SRT), whereas Bosnian Croats rely mostly on media originating in Zagreb. More importantly, when asked what medium they trust more to report the news accurately, most Bosnian Serbs, Croats, and Bosniacs tend to name the source they use most frequently, e.g., the media controlled by their ethnic group.

All the actions taken in late summer and fall 1997, however, only partially addressed the issues hindering an information campaign effective beyond force protection issues. The following are some of the key gaps as of December 1997.

---

press supports the SDA view that there can be no lasting peace until the international community enforces all aspects of the DPA on the Bosnian Croats and Bosnian Serbs. Conversely, until the summer of 1997, most RS press supported the SDS claim that it the party represents the people's interests and backed every trick the party used to not implement the DPA. Several media watchdogs compile extensive data on the local media's coverage of local events. See for example the Bosnian Media Monitoring Report from the Institute of War and Peace Reporting (London) and Media Plan (Sarajevo). Information available at maiser@iwpr.org.uk and warreport@iwpr.org.uk

[153] U.S. Information Agency, "Media Usage in Bosnia Divides Along Ethnic Lines," *Opinion Analysis*, M-138-97, 19 August 1997.

- Reassess the limitations on PI and PSYOP. The international community might never be able to leave a peaceful Bosnia unless it helps the ethnic groups reach some level of reconciliation. Part of this requires unleashing the "non-lethal weapons" of PI and PSYOP against those inhibiting this progress. The PI and PSYOP should be tasked to assume a more proactive and more aggressive posture. Two key elements of such a posture are to make it clear to the people of Bosnia that their nationalistic leaders are an impediment to the Dayton peace process and to resumption of a normal, peaceful life; and to tackle difficult and controversial issues such as the propaganda that led to the nationalistic uprising in the first place. This, however, cannot effectively occur without a clearer conception of the operation's goals and of the international community's end state.
- Focus on an end state rather than an end date. NATO's presence in Bosnia continues to rely on a date of departure (end date) rather than a situation which would allow force departure (end state). Without the political leadership providing an articulated concept for a viable end state, the PSYOP task force will have difficulty creating a cohesive, relevant, and credible campaign.
- Reintegrate PI and PSYOP into the command group: Under Admirals Smith and Lopez, the PIO had very high standing in the staff and frequent (often private) meetings with the admirals (COMIFOR). Similarly, the CJIICTF commander had direct access to COMIFOR or COMARRC whenever required. The situation, however, changed when LANDCENT assumed command of operations. The CPIO and

COMCJICTF access to the commander progressively deteriorated until, by mid-1997, neither had easy access to the commander outside formal meetings. This is an indication of the lower status and importance of these organizations inside the HQ. With CIMIC elements, PI and PSYOP are two of the most important tools for NATO to affect the situation on the ground. They cannot be effective tools while keeping the PIO and COMCJICTF out of planning, for the 10 July 1997 provide clear evidence of the problems that this remoteness can cause. Such a lack of access left both PI and PSYOP in a reactive rather than proactive mode.

Chapter 7:
Identifying Lessons
from the Bosnia
Experience

The NATO experience with public information and psychological operations in *Operations Joint Endeavour* and *Joint Guard* suggest several important lessons for future operations in Bosnia-Herzegovina and elsewhere. Before embarking on this lessons, we should recall the importance of information activities in peace operations. Their importance derives from several factors, which include the following:

- Media reporting plays a critical role in determining the success or failure of a peace operation, as it provides the basis for the public as well as the political elites' opinions. The PI provides the key interlocutor between the operations and these reporters. An effective PI team will diminish the likelihood of unjustified or inaccurate representations of the operation by misinformed or angered journalists.
- In many operations other than war (OOTW), including peace operations, the attitude of the local populace is a critical factor to support mission success.

As with journalists, information activities (with PSYOP in the lead) are the commander's tool for communicating with this population and for encouraging a positive attitude toward the mission's objectives amongst the locals.

- When dealing with interpersonal or interorganizational relations, perception often is as important as (if not more important than) reality. In traditional combat operations, it is (relatively) straightforward to count tanks destroyed or determine the front lines. In OOTW (again, including peace operations), the situation is rarely ever so clear—perceptions are key. A commander's information activities (PI, PSYOP, and civil information) are perhaps the best tools to influence perceptions (internationally and locally) in support of mission objectives.

With these factors in mind, the following paragraphs highlight some of the key lessons identified in the experience of information activities during the first 20 months of NATO operations in Bosnia-Herzegovina.

Clearly Articulated PI Principles and Guidelines

Clarity of guidance is a principle that all military commanders understand. General Joulwan and Admiral Smith provided clear and straightforward guidance for their PI officers to follow. These principles (complete, accurate, and timely reporting) lay at the core of PI activities throughout *Operations Joint Endeavour* and *Joint Guard*. The success of these principles highlights two points. Just as elsewhere in the operational planning, a commander must pay attention to what he expects from his PI officers and must provide guidance so that they can achieve what he expects. In addition, these specific principles well served the military force and NATO overall through the period analyzed. Absent overriding imperatives to the contrary, these specific principles should lie at the core of all military PI activity.

Adapt PI to the Speed of Media Reporting

Technological advances have combined with concepts of media professionalism to greatly diminish the time it takes for something to happen and for the world to have access to reporting (accurate or otherwise) about those events. While technology has similarly affected the military's ability to move information, the military's approach to processing information has not changed in a similar manner. For the PI (and rest of the force) to effectively deal with the reality of today's (and tomorrow's) journalism, several steps seem key:

Establish a chain of information: The military process of information is often too slow to keep up with the fast speed of media reporting. A functional chain of information helps speed up the information flow between subordinate and higher headquarters and allows PI to provide the media with timely information.

Delegate release authority downward: A military commander cannot have an effective public information campaign if he must seek national approval before opening his mouth. The best approach is to establish the parameters within which the commander is allowed to speak. The broader these parameters, the more effective the public information campaign will be in dealing with fast-breaking news.

Strengthen Psychological Operations

Psychological operations contribute to OOTW in several ways. By communicating the appropriate message, a PSYOP campaign can enhance force protection and help convince the local population to support the operation's final objective. To effectively contribute to mission accomplishment requires that several conditions be met:

Tackle difficult and controversial issues: Avoiding the difficult issues in a PSYOP campaign seems to point to two routes: simply delaying facing the inevitable or hindering mission accomplishment by avoiding doing what the mission requires. PSYOP campaigns should not shy away from tackling difficult issues, even if initial messages might have to obliquely or delicately handle such controversial issues.

Undermine adverse propaganda: The military force (and its civilian partners) will not be the only actors on the ground. If it is a conflict, near conflict, or post-conflict situation, it is likely that other parties will be using media and other propaganda tools to spread a message counter to the international community's interests. The

PSYOP force should provide the key military element to deal with such elements: tracking, analyzing, and countering these propaganda efforts.

Back messages with action: Messages should be tied to concrete action. Constantly reemphasizing messages that do not comport with reality (such as talking of freedom of movement in Bosnia-Herzegovina when every local was nervous about traveling into another ethnic group's territory) will undercut credibility, which is what lies at the heart of a successful information campaign.

Adapt to Local Audiences

In OOTW, winning the hearts and minds of the local population is important. As with any other type of operation, a commander's goal is to avoid local population interference with operations. But in a peace operation where the use of force is limited, persuading the locals to support the operation and potentially using it to apply pressure on uncooperative local authorities will enhance mission accomplishment. To improve the odds that the local population will accept the message, the campaign must be adapted to the local audiences. The following are three steps to achieve this.

Tailor the message appropriately. The PSYOP operation must tailor its message to local audiences' knowledge and culture. In addition, dissemination needs to fit the locals' media consumption habits.

PI should not neglect local media. PI officers typically focus on international and national publics (their primary and most important audiences). This focus, however, should not be at the expense of local journalists, especially when they are the primary source of information for the local population (as was the case in Bosnia). To reinforce the PSYOP campaign, the PI operation needs to take into account the requirements and needs of local journalists.

Use the force to communicate with locals. To a large extent, any soldier's interaction with the locals can be used to foster the commander's goals. Force posture sends a message. Daily interactions between the soldiers and the local population can be used to disseminate further the commander's message.

Associate PI, PSYOP, and Civil Information

To increase their effectiveness, closely associate information activities. The close association between PI, PSYOP, and civil information should aim at coordinating and synchronizing the messages so they reinforce each other. If the PSYOP campaign is engaged in grey or black propaganda, however, this close association could become inappropriate.

Integrate PI/PSYOP with Command Group and Establish Close Relations with Commander

The PIO and PSYOP commander cannot be fully effective without a close relationship with the commanding general. From the earliest stages, these officers must be strongly established as key actors in the command group. Commanders should assure strong ties with these key non-lethal weapons. This could involve, for example, holding daily (small) information meetings as well as direct access to the commander.

Coordinate Internally

Fully effective information activities are tied into the operations. Close integration with other operational staffs (in particular the "3" shop) allows information activities to be used effectively to prepare for and better respond to contingencies and to refocus the effort when necessary. To achieve such level of integration requires internal coordination whereby PI, PSYOP, and civil information hold regular meetings with operational staffs to receive their inputs on the information campaign and channel feedback into the headquarters. The creation of PI and PSYOP liaisons to the JOC during IFOR operations is an example of a beneficial coordination mechanism.

Coordinate Externally

The military is not the only actor in OOTW. In peace operations, the military will work alongside civilian international organizations such as the United Nations, the High Commissioner for Refugees, and the World Bank. Coordinating, cooperating, and working with these organizations will enhance overall mission effectiveness and speed mission achievement. Information activities is one of the areas which will gain with such cooperation.

Improve PSYOP-civilian cooperation: Mutual ignorance and reluctance make establishing coordination between PSYOP forces and civilian organizations a difficult process. Successful coordination requires that PSYOP familiarize itself with how international organizations operate, determine how best it can support their missions, and establish a good liaison with international organizations.

Learn from IFOR PI-civilian organization successes: In the PI arena, IFOR/SFOR external coordination is a template for future operations. With two simple mechanisms (combined briefings with a pre-briefing meeting), the PIO established a successful relationship that benefited both the military and civilian organizations. Future commanders can capitalize on this success.

Clearly Articulate an End State

Like every other element of an operation, information activities' effectiveness will be hampered (if not crippled) if the political leadership cannot (and does not) clearly articulate a concept for the mission's end state. The absence of a clear end state makes it more difficult to develop a successful information strategy. To develop a convincing and credible position, the PSYOP and PI need to have a clear objective in mind, so they can work backwards to develop the necessary steps leading to the final objective. A viable end state is fundamental both as the objective which helps to define a strategy and as a measure of success or failure for the mission. Without an idea of where they are supposed to be heading, no element of information activities will be fully effective in their endeavours.

These lessons do not necessarily constitute a blueprint for success. However, adopting the lessons identified from the Bosnia experience (both the positive and negative experiences) will make future U.S. and multinational peace operations more effective and more likely to achieve mission objectives.

Appendix 1:
Local and International Responsibilities in the General Framework Agreement for Peace Implementation

The following two tables summarize the responsibilities of the entities (the Federation and the Bosnian-Serb Republic) of Bosnia-Herzegovina and of the international community in the implementation of the General Framework Agreement for Peace. The first table lays out the responsibilities specifically mentioned in the agreement. The second table presents the international organizations that have come to play an important role in the implementation process, even though they are not mentioned in the Dayton Agreement.

Table 1: Summary of the General Framework Agreement for Peace Responsibilities

Annex	Mission	Lead agency and role
1A: Military aspects of the Peace Settlement.	Separate the factions and create the conditions of a durable cessation of hostilities.	- Parties uphold the cease-fire. - NATO ensures continued compliance with the provisions of annex 1A (use of force authorized if necessary). - ICRC facilitates the exchange of prisoners.
1B: Regional stabilization	Regional arms control stabilization.	Entities negotiate force reduction and regional military balance under OSCE auspices.
2: Agreement on IEBL and related issues	Establishes the boundary between the Federation and the Bosnian-Serb Republic. Outlines Brcko arbitration.	- NATO authorizes and supervises selective marking of the IEBL and zone of separation (final authority rests with NATO). - Arbitrators (designated by the entities and the international community) issue a binding decision on Brcko within a year.
3: Elections	National and municipal elections in Bosnia-Herzegovina.	OSCE supervises the preparation of and conducts the elections after the entities agree on rules.
4: Constitution of Bosnia-Herzegovina	New constitution of Bosnia-Herzegovina (adopted upon signature of the agreement).	- Entities establish common institutions of BH. - IMF appoints Central Bank Governor.
5: Arbitration	Establishes a system of arbitration between the Federation and the RS for resolving disputes.	- Entities design and implement a system of arbitration.
6: Human Rights	Guarantees human rights in Bosnia-Herzegovina.	- Parties agree to guarantee to all the people of BH the highest level of internationally recognized human rights. - Parties create a commission on Human Rights consisting of an ombudsman and a Council of Human Rights. - OSCE designates the ombudsman - Council of Europe designates several members (including the chairman) of the Council of HR.

Table 1: Summary of the General Framework Agreement for Peace Responsibilities, cont'd.

Annex	Mission	Lead Agency and Role
7: Refugees and Displaced Persons	Return of Refugees and Displaced persons to the location of their choice (including their pre-war settlement).	- Entities create the conditions for peaceful and orderly returns. - UNHCR develops a repatriation plan in consultation with asylum countries and the parties. - European Court of HR appoints chair of Commission for Refugees and DPs. - IO/NGOs monitor human rights and humanitarian conditions in the country - Parties assist the ICRC in its effort to determine the whereabouts of persons unaccounted for.
8: Commission to Preserve National Monuments	Preservation of monuments and historic sites.	- Parties create a commission to preserve monuments & historic sites. - UNESCO appoints several members to the commission (including its chairman).
9: Establishment of BH Public Corporations	Reconstruction of economic infrastructure.	- Entities establish a commission on public corporations. - EBRD designates two members (including the chairman).
10: Civilian Implementation of the Peace Settlement	Coordination of international civilian and local government efforts in support of peace accord implementation.	OHR monitors implementation, maintains close contact with the parties to promote their full compliance and coordinate the activities of the International community.
11: International Police Force	Local police force.	IPTF monitors and inspects law enforcement activities and facilities, advises and trains local police.

Table 2: Implementing Agencies with an Official Role (Not Mentioned in the GFAP) [154]

Agencies	Origin of Mandate	Principle Role in Supporting Sustainable Peace
IMG	UNHCR (1994)	Coordinates and manages international economic initiatives for reconstruction of infrastructure.
ECMM	European Union	Provides timely information to capitals of the European Community.
WFP	UN General Assembly	Maintains food supplies for relief, without impairing local food markets.
FAO	UN General Assembly	Supports economic development by encouraging balanced reconstruction and international investment to meet local needs.
UNICEF	UN General Assembly	Meets the physical, social, and educational needs of children.
ICG	OHR	Supports OHR with analysis and liaison.
UNHCR	UN General Assembly	Monitors and reports on human rights situation.

---

[154] This table is reproduced from David Last, *Implementing the Dayton Accords: the Challenges of Inter-Agency Coordination*, Paper presented at Cornwallis II: Analysis of and for Conflict Resolution, Pearson Peacekeeping Centre, Cornwallis Park, 8-10 April 1997, p 17.

Appendix 2:
Bosnia-Herzegovina as Agreed Upon at Dayton

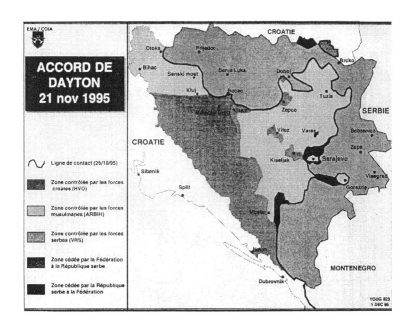

Appendix 3:
Milestones in Implementation of Annex 1A of the General Framework Agreement for Peace

Date	Milestone	Event	Completion
19 Jan 96	D+30	Parties are to withdraw their forces from a zone of separation established on either side of the agreed-upon cease-fire line.	D+30
3 Feb 96	D+45	All Parties' forces are to be withdrawn from the territories to be transferred to other entities.	
19 Mar 96	D+90	Transfer of territory between the entities is completed.	D+90
18 Apr 96	D+120	All heavy weapons are to be placed into IFOR-supervised cantonment sites or otherwise demobilized.	D+180

Appendix 4:
Multinational Divisions
Areas of Responsibility

Acronym List

AFSOUTH:	Allied Forces South
AOR:	Area Of Responsibility
ARRC:	ACE Rapid Reaction Corps
B-H:	Bosnia-Herzegovina
CI:	Civil Information
CIMIC:	Civil-Military Cooperation
CIO:	Chief Information Officer
CJCIMIC:	Combined/Joint Civil-Military Cooperation
CJICTF:	Combined Joint Information Campaign Task Force (SFOR)
CJIICTF:	Combined Joint IFOR Information Campaign Task Force
CMTF:	Civil-Military Task Force
CPIC:	Coalition Press and Information Center
CPIO:	Chief Public Information Officer
COMARRC:	Commander of the ACE Rapid Reaction Corps
COMCJI(I)CTF:	Commander of the CJI(I)CTF
COMIFOR:	Commander of the Implementation Forces
COMSFOR:	Commander of the Stabilization Forces
DPA:	Dayton Peace Agreement (See GFAP)
EBRD:	European Bank for Reconstruction and Development
FWF:	Former Warring Factions
GFAP:	General Framework Agreement for Peace
HQ:	Headquarters
HUMINT:	Human Intelligence
ICRC:	International Committee of the Red Cross
ICTY:	International Criminal Tribunal for former-Yugoslavia
IEBL:	Inter-Entity Boundary Line
IFOR:	Implementation Force
IPTF:	International Police Task Force
JICC:	Joint Information Coordination Committee
JOC:	Joint Operations Center
LANDCENT:	Allied Land Forces Central Europe

LNO:	Liaison Officer
MNDs:	Multi-National Divisions
NAC:	North Atlantic Council
OHR:	Office of the High Representative
OIC:	Officer In Charge
OPCON:	Operational Control
OSCE:	Organization for the Security and Cooperation in Europe
PI:	Public Information
PIO:	Public Information Officer
PSPA:	Peace Support Psychological Activities
PSO:	Peace Support Operation
PSYOP:	Psychological Operations
RS:	Republika Srpska
SACEUR:	Supreme Allied Command Europe
SFOR:	Stabilization Force
SHAPE:	Supreme Headquarters Allied Powers Europe
TACON:	Tactical Control
TOA:	Transfer of Authority
TPT:	Tactical PSYOP Teams
UNHCR:	United Nations High Commissioner for Refugees
UNMIBH:	United Nations Mission in Bosnia-Herzegovina
UNPROFOR:	United Nations Protection Force
ZOS:	Zone of Separation

Glossary of NATO Terminology

CIMIC: Civil-Military Cooperation is defined as "the means by which allied commanders establish and maintain formal relations with the national authorities, populations, international, and non-governmental organizations in their area of interest." Closely related to U.S. Civil Affairs.

CIO: Chief Information Officer. An officer in charge of coordinating all information activities (in particular PI and PSYOP) within the command with operational matters. The author is aware of no U.S. equivalent in recent U.S. military operations.

CJ: NATO staff components. The abbreviation CJ refers to the Combined/Joint nature of NATO staffs in B-H.

CJIICTF: Combined Joint IFOR Information Campaign Task Force: Organization in charge of running the psychological operations during IFOR. No U.S. equivalent.

CJICTF: Combined Joint Information Campaign Task Force. Organization in charge of running the psychological operations campaign during SFOR. No U.S. equivalent.

Information Campaign: Official NATO term for the multimedia campaign designed to influence the attitudes of the people in B-H and shape their behavior in favor of IFOR troops and operations. The information campaign was a psychological operations campaign, but political sensitivities toward the term "PSYOP" prevented the use of the term. The phrase "nformation campaign" was also used at ARRC level to designate the combined and synchronized use of Public Information, Psychological Operations, and Civil-Military Information in support of COMARRC's intent.

PIO: Public Information Officer. Officer in charge of conducting media relations (and to a much lesser extent command information). The PIO is equivalent to a U.S. Public Affairs Officer.

Sources

To write this monograph, the author used a wide range of sources, including official material, books and articles, and interviews with protagonists. The following is an abridged list of the most important references used to support this work.

ON BOSNIA

Official Material

General Framework Agreement for Peace. The full text of the agreement (along with annexes and appendixes) is available on several Websites, including NATO's (http://www.nato.int).

United States General Accounting Office, *Bosnia Peace Operation: Progress Toward Achieving the Dayton Agreement's Goals*, Report to the Chairman, Committee on Foreign Relations, U.S. Senate, GAO/NSIAD-97-132, Washington, D.C., Mary 1997.

IFOR and OHR reports to UNSC. Every month (for IFOR/SFOR) and every three months (for the OHR), both organizations reported to the United Nations Security

Council. These reports are available on the UN Websites (http://www.un.org).

Books and Articles

Christopher Bennett, *Yugoslavia Bloody Collapse: Causes, Courses, Consequences*, London, C. Hurst & Co, 1995.

Stephen Carr-Smith, "Bosnia - One Year on From Dayton," *The Officer*, March-April 1997, pp. 50-53.

Jean Cot, "Ex-Yougoslavie: Une paix bâclée," *Défense Nationale*, July1997, pp. 71-82.

Loup Francart, "La prévention: Une exigence conceptuelle et opérationnelle," *Les Cahiers de la Fondations pour les Etudes de Défense*, nb 8, 1997, pp. 51-58.

Richard Holbrooke, "The Road to Sarajevo," *The New Yorker*, 21-28 October 1996.

Gordada Igric, "Relectures guerrières de l'histoire yougoslave," *Le Monde Diplomatique*, September 1995.

David Last, "Implementing the Dayton Accords: The Challenges of Inter-Agency Coordination," paper presented for Cornwallis II: Analysis of and for Conflict Resolution, Pearson Peacekeeping Centre, Cornwallis Park, 8-10 April 1997.

Peter Mass, *Love Thy Neighbor: A Story of War*, New York, Alfred knopf, 1996.

David Owen, *Balkan Odyssey*, London, Indigo Editions, 1996.

Laura Silber, Allan Little, *The Death of Yugoslavia*, London, Penguin Books, 1996.

Susan Woodward, "Bosnia," *The Brookings Review*, vol. 15, nb 2, Spring 1997.

ON INFORMATION

Official Material

NATO, *NATO Doctrine for Peace Support Operations*, NATO UNCLASSIFIED, Brussels, draft, 20 October 1993.

SHAPE, *ACE Directive 95-1: ACE Public Information Operations*, NATO UNCLASSIFIED, Mons, 22 August 1996.

NATO, *Bi-MNC Directive for NATO Doctrine for Peace Support Operations*, PfP UNCLASSIFIED, Brussels, 11 December 1995.

NATO, *NATO Psychological Operations Policy*, NATO UNCLASSIFIED, Brussels, 21 March 1997.

Department of the Army, *Field Manuel, FM 46-1: Public Affairs Operations*, Washington D.C., November 1996.

Department of the Army, *Field Manual, FM 33-1: Psychological Operations*, Washington D.C., February 1993.

Joint Chiefs of Staff, *Joint Pub 3-13: Joint Doctrine for Information Operations*, Washington, D.C., 21 January 1997.

U.K. Ministry of Defence, Working Arrangements with the Media in Times of Emergency, Tension, Conflict or War (the "Green Book"), London, no date.

Books and Articles

Stephen Badsey, Modern Military Operations and the Media, Camberley, UK, Strategic and Combat Studies Institute, Occasional Paper nb 8, 1994.

Renaud de la Brosse, "Les voix de la guerre", in Jean Cot (dir), *Dernière guerre balkanique? Ex-Yougoslavie : témoignages, analyses, perspectives*, Paris, L'Harmattan, 1996.

Stanco Ceroic, "L'information est-elle possible face à la propagande ?" *Dialogues et Documents pour le progrès de l'homme/Expériences et réflexions sur la reconstruction nationale et la paix*, Documents de travail de la Fondation pour le progrès de l'homme, nb 64, p. 190.

Capt. Stuart Gordon, "United Nations PR: The Short Straw?" *Despatches: The Journal of the Territorial Army Pool of Public Information Officers*, nb 6, Spring 1996, pp. 166-171.

Nik Gowing, "The Tyranny of Real-Time", *Despatches: The Journal of the Territorial Army Pool of Public Information Officers*, nb 6, Spring 1996, pp. 61-64.

Françoise J. Hampton, *Incitement and the Media Responsibility of and for the Media in the Conflicts in the Former-Yugoslavia*, Papers in the Theory and Practice of Human Rights, University of Essex, nb 3, 1993.

Catherine Humblot, "La manipulation de la mémoire," *Le Monde*, 22 July 1993.

Maj. Gen. Kiszely, UKA, Interview to *Jane's Defense Weekly*, 18 December 1996, p. 32.

Martin Libicki, *What is Information Warfare?* Washington, D.C., National Defense University, Institute for National Strategic Studies, August 1995.

Henri Madelin, "Information et idéologie, Télévisions en guerre," *Le Monde Diplomatique*, October 1990.

Glyn Mathias, "Television Can Sway Events", *Despatches: The Journal of the Territorial Army Pool of Public Infor-*

mation Officers, nb 5, Spring 1995, pp. 39-42.

Tadeusz Mazowiecki, *Rapport spécial sur les médias,* rapport préparé pour la Commission des Droits de l'Homme des Nations Unies, E/CN 4/1995/54, 13 décembre 1994.

General Gordon Sullivan, Colonel James M. Dubick, *War in the Information Age,* Carlisle Barracks, Strategic Studies Institute, 6 June 1994.

Gordon Sullivan, Anthony M. Coroalles, *The Army in the Information Age,* Carlisle Barracks, Strategic Studies Institute, 31 March 1995.

Maj. Jerry Sullivan, "The Reserve's Commitment to Special Operations," *Army,* vol. 47, nb 4, April 1997, pp. 24-27.

I. Trainor, "Yugoslavia's Brutal Television War," *International Press Institute Report,* vol. 41, nb 2, February 1992.

INTERVIEWS

Knowledge of the particularities of Bosnia operations was further acquired during two observation missions conducted in Bosnia in October 1996 and March-April 1997, during which the author interviewed nearly one hundred protagonists. The following are some of these interviews: Capt. Bailey, USA, IFOR Information Campaign LNO to MND (SE); LTC Brook, UKA, MND (SW) chief PIO; LTC Brune, USA, CJCIMIC Chief Civil Information; Mr. Bullivan, OHR press and public affairs officer; Maj. Caruso, USA, SFOR Information Campaign S3; Ms. Cepeda, Director, OSCE voter education department. Alan Davis, Programs Officer, Institute for War and Peace Reporting, London; Mrs. Dawson, OSCE public affairs officer; Col. Dell'Aria, FRA, MND (SE) Chief PIO; Capt. Feliu, USA, IFOR PIO, LNO to the JOC; Mr. Foley, OSCE spokesman; LTC Furlong, USA, Deputy Commander

IFOR Information Campaign; Staff Sergeant Helton, USAR, SFOR CMTF PAO; LTC Hoehne, SHAPE PIO, media chief; Col. Icenogle, USA, MND (N) JIB director; Mr. Ivanko, UNMIBH spokesman; Mr. Janowski, UNHCR spokesman; Mr. Jolidon, Civ, COMARRC media advisor; Joe Kazlas, Director, OSCE media development; Maj. Marconnet, FR Gen, MND (SE) PIO; LTC John Markham, USA, SHAPE PSYOP staff officer; Maj. Mason, USA, editor *The Herald of Peace*; Col. Moitie, FRA, COMFRANCE chief PIO; LTC Morger, SHAPE PIO, plans and policy; Maj. Moyers, USA, CPIC IFOR media chief; Col. Mulvey, USA, Chief LANDCENT PIO; Mr. Murphy, OHR spokesman; Col. Nimo, NA, MND (N) CPIC director; Col. de Noirmont, FRA, Deputy Chief IFOR PIO; Maj. Oliver, IFOR Information Campaign Product Development; Sergeant Panzer, SFOR Information Campaign LNO to international organizations; Mr. Philips, Chief media operations, Permanent Joint Headquarters, United Kingdom; Ms. Quentier, UNHCR spokesman for Mostar; Col. Rausch, USA, Chief SFOR PIO; Col. Robey, UKA, SFOR chief information officer; Col. Schoenhaus, USAR, SFOR Information Campaign commander; Col. Serveille, FRA, Deputy Chief IFOR PIO; Pierre Servent, Media relation advisor to the French Minister of Defense; Maj. Smith, USA, SFOR Information Campaign product development chief; Patrick Svenson, UNMIBH deputy spokesman; Capt. Van Dyke, USN, Chief IFOR PIO; Sylva Vujovic, Programs Officer, Media Plan, Sarajevo; Mrs. Weltz, SFOR Information Campaign strategic analyst; Col. Wilton, UKA, ARRC Chief Information Officer.

About the Author

Pascale Combelles Siegel is an independent researcher based in Arlington, Virginia, where she works on media and defense issues. She has worked with Evidence Based Research, Inc. since fall 1996, focusing on the subject matter of this monograph. In support of NDU, Mrs. Siegel directed the NATO Joint Analysis Team's lessons learned analysis of public information and information campaign during IFOR operations and participated in analysis of Civil-Military Cooperation during the first four months of SFOR operations. Mrs. Siegel's work on military-media issues has appeared in books and journals on both sides of the Atlantic. She is currently completing her dissertation, which is entitled "Ideological Conflict and Practical Reliance: The U.S. military-media relationship in times of conflict since Grenada."

Order Form

We hope you enjoy your complimentary copy of this CCRP publication. The publications listed on the reverse side of this form are available at no cost through CCRP. Simply mark the publication(s) you would like to receive and return these sheets to the following address:

CCRP Publications Distribution Center
c/o Evidence Based Research, Inc.
1595 Spring Hill Road, Suite 250
Vienna, VA 22182

☐   Please send me the publications I have marked.
☐   Please remove my name from your mailing list.
☐   Please change my listing in your database.

Name _____

Title _____

Company _____

Address _____

City _____ State _____ Zip _____

Phone _____

E-mail _____

Area(s) of Expertise _____

I would like to see more publications on the following subject(s):

I use these publications primarily for the following reason(s):
☐   Personal reference   ☐   Course textbook
☐   Work reference   ☐   I don't read these books

For further information on CCRP, please visit our Website at
http://www.dodccrp.org.

CCRP Publications

Command and Control

- ☐ Coalition Command and Control (Maurer)
- ☐ Command, Control, and the Common Defense (Allard)
- ☐ Command and Control in Peace Operations Workshop
- ☐ Command Arrangements for Peace Operations (Alberts & Hayes)*
- ☐ Complexity, Global Politics, and National Security (Alberts & Czerwinski, eds.)

Information Technologies and Information Warfare

- ☐ Defending Cyberspace and Other Metaphors (Libicki)*
- ☐ Defensive Information Warfare (Alberts)*
- ☐ Dominant Battlespace Knowledge (Johnson & Libicki)*
- ☐ The Information Age: An Anthology on Its Impacts and Consequences (Papp & Alberts, eds.)*
- ☐ Information Warfare and International Law (Kuehl, ed.)
- ☐ The Mesh and the Net: Speculations on Armed Conflict in a Time of Free Silicon (Libicki)
- ☐ Second International C2 Research & Technology Symposium Proceedings Document
- ☐ Standards: The Rough Road to the Common Byte (Libicki)*
- ☐ Proceedings of the Third International Symposium on C2 Research & Technology
- ☐ The Unintended Consequences of Information Age Technologies (Alberts)*
- ☐ What is Information Warfare? (Libicki)*

Operations Other Than War

- ☐ Interagency and Political-Military Dimensions of Peace Operations: Haiti - a Case Study (Daly Hayes & Wheatley, eds.)
- ☐ Joint Training for Information Managers (Maxwell)*
- ☐ Lessons from Bosnia: The IFOR Experience (Wentz, ed.)
- ☐ NGOs and the Military in the Interagency Process (Davidson, Landon, & Daly Hayes)
- ☐ Operations Other Than War*
- ☐ Shock and Awe: Achieving Rapid Dominance (Ullman & Wade)*
- ☐ Target Bosnia: Integrating International Information Activities in Bosnia-Herzegovina

* Published in conjunction with the NDU Press.